Microverses

Microverses

*Observations from a
Shattered Present*

Dylan Riley

VERSO
London • New York

First published by Verso 2022
© Dylan Riley 2022
Earlier versions of some of the texts appeared
in *New Left Review* or *Sidecar* 2021

The moral rights of the author have been asserted

1 3 5 7 9 10 8 6 4 2

Verso
UK: 6 Meard Street, London W1F 0EG
US: 388 Atlantic Avenue, Brooklyn, NY 11217
versobooks.com

Verso is the imprint of New Left Books

ISBN-13: 978-1-83976-840-8
ISBN-13: 978-1-83976-841-5 (UK EBK)
ISBN-13: 978-1-83976-842-2 (US EBK)

British Library Cataloguing in Publication Data
A catalogue record for this book is available from the British Library

Library of Congress Cataloging-in-Publication Data

Names: Riley, Dylan J., 1971– author.
Title: Microverses : observations from a shattered present / Dylan Riley.
Description: Brooklyn, NY : Verso Books, 2022. | Includes bibliographical
    references and index.
Identifiers: LCCN 2022018212 (print) | LCCN 2022018213 (ebook) | ISBN
    9781839768408 (paperback) | ISBN 9781839768422 (ebk)
Subjects: LCSH: Social sciences—Philosophy—History—21st century. |
    Social problems—History—21st century. | Sociologists—History. |
    COVID-19 Pandemic, 2020—Social aspects.
Classification: LCC H61 .R4957 2022 (print) | LCC H61 (ebook) | DDC
    300.1—dc23/eng/20220602
LC record available at https://lccn.loc.gov/2022018212
LC ebook record available at https://lccn.loc.gov/2022018213

Typeset in Sabon by MJ & N Gavan, Truro, Cornwall
Printed and bound by CPI Group (UK) Ltd, Croydon CR0 4YY

Ad Emanuela, l'amore della mia vita

Contents

Preface

What are they? Pieces of thought originating in a context that combined an epochal social and political crisis—the Covid pandemic and the last months of Trump—with a shattering personal one, my wife Emanuela's illness. In a way, they are attempts to deal with these hammer blows, intellectually and therapeutically. Each note was written first with pen and paper in a notebook and then again on a computer, without further emendation. This method of composition, which I found strangely liberating, was partially dictated by the massive disruption of normal routine. Writing by hand was initially a strategy to give myself a break from hours spent on Zoom; it became a necessity as medical visits rendered long sessions at my desk impossible. Indeed, many of the notes were sketched out in parking lots or waiting rooms. These conditions allowed me, quite unintentionally, to avoid a common trap of computer-mediated writing. Just as the malleability of oils may draw the painter into a cycle of self-destructive correction, so the ease of revision on a computer can tempt the writer to overwork, and thereby destroy the initial thought. Writing just two drafts, in different media, guarded me against this. A second particularity of these pieces is that they could not rely on much formal apparatus of citations or references; rarely did I have any texts open when composing them. This forced me to write with a pared-down directness, the advantages of which hopefully outweigh the dangers.

A few further words might be useful to contextualize what follows. The notes were written over a period of a little more than a year. The first dates to my forty-ninth birthday, March 25, 2020; the last, on representation, to October 3, 2021. They begin accordingly in the first weeks of the pandemic "lockdown" in the United States, extend through the early months of the Biden administration, and are roughly bisected by the January 6 "insurrection" at the Capitol. Over this span I worked at an uneven pace. After an initial rush of reflections mostly concerned with the politics and experience of the early pandemic, there was a hiatus broken at note 9, produced on December 23. Between these dates (March and December 2020) the second of the two crises (Emanuela's diagnosis) intervened; this partly explains the gap, and is doubtless also responsible for the tone of much of the later writing. From that point on I wrote at a fairly regular clip of about twenty pieces a month, until they ultimately tapered off as the dislocation of routine which was their condition of possibility began to ease.

Now, then, seems like a natural time to collect them, even if I hope to return to this form—to which I have become very attached—in the future. An overly ambitious book project stands for the present between me and any new such notes.

Thematically the notes mostly range over three areas: politics in the broad sense (including both electoral politics and political culture); personal experience; and sociology. Flanking these are two topics which are the focus of just a few notes, the pandemic and the status of the collection as it was being compiled. There was a shift in the weight of specific subjects, particularly within the political theme, over the course of the writing. While presidential politics looms large in the early notes, after January 2021 it mostly drops out. Only two notes (61 and 79) attempt a characterization of the Biden government. This reflects in part my own uncertainty about the nature of the incoming administration. Biden ran a strategically shrewd but substantively empty campaign; in office, all that is so far clear is that his domestic agenda will express the balance of sharply opposed forces within the Democratic "Party" (a strange noun to apply to such a political formation), and little of his own meager stock of ideas.

What of their form? For the most part the notes are written in the idiom of what C. Wright Mills termed "classical social analysis"—Durkheim, Gramsci, Hayek, Marx, Lukács, and Weber loom large in them—although I have tried to express my ideas with a minimum of specialized terminology. One sort of note uses theoretical language to describe ephemeral, routine experiences, hopefully casting them in a new light and revealing connections that might not otherwise be obvious. Another sort explores theoretical issues more directly, presenting key issues and problems in a highly compressed form designed to force central debates to the fore. Not by any means finished arguments, their wager is that it might be possible to draw lessons of broad theoretical import from "individual experience," and vice versa to illuminate experience through the language of social theory.*

Such a venture is likely to appear anachronistic today. For the idea of sociology as a creative linking of lived experience and theory—in Mills's terms, "biography and history"—seems largely moribund. The idea, central to the classical tradition, that experience only becomes such when mediated by theoretical categories, is alien to contemporary sensibilities attuned to the honoring, recovering, and recognizing of experience rather than to its realization through "critique." There is of course a rich tradition of books in this

---

* "Society is essentially the substance of the individual. For this reason, social analysis can learn incomparably more from individual experience than Hegel conceded": Theodor Adorno, *Minima Moralia: Reflections from a Damaged Life* (London and New York: Verso Books, 2005), p. 17.

classical vein: Adorno's *Minima Moralia,* Du Bois's numerous autobiographies, and Mills's *Sociological Imagination,* for instance. Yet today, the "sociology" section of a quality bookstore is unlikely to contain much in the way of new examples of the genre. Few readers would be foolish enough to look for a guide to living or an intellectual therapeutic among the odd jumble of texts collected under that rubric.

The notes that follow make no pretense of offering an introduction of any sort to the "discipline of sociology" or, even more narrowly, "social theory." Instead, they try to recover what I see as sociology's most decisive potential contribution: its point of view. The sociological perspective, as I understand it, takes the totality of social existence as its object, rather than constituting itself in relationship to a specific layer or subsystem. For sociology, as for Hegel, "the true is the whole." Three features follow from this: sociology should be historical and comparative; counterphenomenal; and theoretical. The historical character of sociology becomes plain as soon as it is recognized that all specifically sociological problems take the form of the question, Why does a given set of social arrangements operate in a particular way, rather than another? The analysis of any such problem requires an explanation of the genesis of the relations in question, and a comparative framework specifying why the relations emerged in one instance, but not others. When these basic points are grasped, one can readily appreciate that all sociological studies are historical comparative studies of social forms, even when their authors—as is very often the case—are not fully aware of this fact. Sociology is counterphenomenal because its raison d'être as a specialized language and form of analysis is that the connections that link the social totality are not immediately obvious. It is also intrinsically theoretical: if there were no need for theory, there would be no need for sociology.

What is the connection between totalization and critique? In sociology the term "critique" has come to mean the discussion of values.* This makes "critical sociology" seem like a special form of sociology, close to philosophy or political theory. In my view, however, critique is far more integral to the enterprise of social analysis than this position implies. It refers, most generally, to an elucidation of the conditions of possibility for something to exist, and more specifically, an explanation of the conditions under which certain claims, or even whole styles of reasoning, are valid. Marx's "critique of political economy," for example, explains the social conditions under which use values take on exchange values, and simultaneously the conditions under which political economy provides a relatively adequate analysis.

But "critique" in this sense is hardly specific to Marxism: it characterizes every form of sociology, and particularly sociology's relationship to other parts of the syllabus. Political sociology is among other things a "critique" of procedural democracy, in the sense that it identifies the structures of political expropriation that make voting the primary expression of political struggle. Weber's economic sociology is to a large degree a "critique" of marginalism in the same sense that Marx's work is a critique of political economy. Barbara Fields's work is a "critique" of race in that it shows how racial ideology constitutes the historical condition of possibility for races. Feminists have cashed out in various ways the observation that the division of the world into genders constitutes the basis of women's oppression. It is a critique of female subjugation in the sense that it focuses on establishing the preconditions of that subjugation. In each of these domains, the specifically sociological moment is totalization: the reinsertion of the immediate

---

*   Michael Burawoy defines critical sociology as "a dialogue about ends": "For Public Sociology," in Dan Clawson, et al., eds., *Public Sociology: Fifteen Eminent Sociologists Debate Politics and the Profession in the Twenty-First Century* (Berkeley: University of California Press, 2007), p. 34.

phenomenon into the socio-historical context that makes it possible. This is why totalization is the precondition of critique, and it is also why "critical sociology" is not one type of sociology, it *is* sociology—even if this is not always, or even usually, made explicit.

Totalizing, historicizing, theoretical: obviously the entire enterprise of sociology, as I understand it, is closely related to Marxism (to which it constitutes an alternative, or supplement, depending on one's perspective). What, then, is the relationship of these notes to Marxism itself, sociology's urantagonist? Marxism's two main twentieth-century revivals, in the twenties and sixties, were both marked by a productive cross-fertilization with sociology: think of Lukács's engagement with Weber, and Althusser's obvious debt to Durkheim. The current resurgence of Marxism shows very little sign of this, apart from trivial linguistic borrowings such as "cultural capital," largely because the concerns of contemporary social theory have little relevance to socialist politics.

This lack of engagement comes with costs. The main one is that the new socialist and progressive literature relies heavily on essentially legalistic concepts in its mode of social analysis. The consequence for contemporary left thought is a pervasive and uncontrolled circulation of pre-Marxian and presociological ideas: "justice," "fairness," "equality," and so on. Marxism becomes, from this perspective, a kind of left-Rawlsianism, while socialism is reduced to the demand for "fair" distribution. But the specificity of Marxism is that it provides an intellectual framework that does not rely on such concepts. Instead, historical materialism emphasizes the contradictory character of all social forms, and particularly of capitalism. Its basic demand is not for a fair, or just, society; rather, it is for a way of living together in which the human species as a whole is at least partially liberated from second nature: its own alienated sociality. Perhaps this could best be termed a "humanized society." Only when this project comes back into focus will neosocialism lose its defensive and legalistic posture, and begin once again to pose itself as a solution to some of our basic problems.

These notes, then, are an invitation to think about the activity of social theory in a different way. If there is a thread linking all of them, it is the fundamental connectedness of human experience. In my opinion this is the basic lesson of social theory, and it seems to me the first step to the construction of a slightly less inhuman world than the one we currently inhabit.

Acknowledgments

I owe more than the usual thanks to the intellectual generosity and exacting standards of Perry Anderson and Susan Watkins. It was Susan who pushed me to continue producing these notes, even when I was a bit doubtful, and Perry encouraged me to collect them as well as providing incisive comments throughout. Thanks are also due to Robert Brenner, Michael Burawoy, and Christopher Muller, who all saw several of the pieces and provided me helpful feedback on them, even if they perhaps felt the entire enterprise to be a bit odd. My brothers, Evan and Scott, and my parents also read and reacted to them, each providing both encouragement and critique. (Evan was particularly insistent about the distinction between "facts" and "statements of fact," which I had slurred over in the initial *New Left Review* publication of the notes.) Graham Teaford and Zulema Valdez were lively interlocutors, while John Connelly, Rebecca Emigh, and Sandra Susan Smith gave me moral support throughout. Edwin Ackerman, Jonah Stuart Brundage, Adrian Grama, and William Welsh provided searching critiques of the preface. Finally, my partner Emanuela read and commented on every note, proposed several ideas, and was a severe yet generous critic. It is to her that I dedicate this small volume.

Microverses

Antigovernmentality. How to understand the current inflection point? In one of his many attempts to grasp the specificity of modern rule, Foucault describes a historical transition from "discipline" to "governmentality." The latter focuses on masses and averages, not on individuals. It works through the nudging of behavior to produce collectively desirable outcomes. But something bizarre is happening now. The US response to the coronavirus seems to involve a complete breakdown of this model: an unraveling of governmentality.

Leave aside Trump's inane rantings, and focus instead on the experts: Fauci and others. How do they conceive of the purpose of testing for the virus? For them tests should be administered to persons who display symptoms in order to confirm whether the individuals in question have the virus. This shows that even among medical experts there is confusion about the object of the test. For clearly the point of testing is not to determine the health or sickness of the individual, but rather to grasp the incidence of the disease in the population—not to ask the clinical question "Is this person infected?" but the epidemiological question "What is the rate of disease in the population?" The confusion between the two reveals the unravelling of governmentality. For the latter question, of course, it is just as important to test the healthy and the asymptomatic as it is to test the sick. What is the source of this confusion? Possibly the expression of an individualism so intensely heightened by the long neoliberal counterrevolution that the very concept of "population" has been blurred? It is not just that public health is neglected, underfunded, degraded. It is also that the very object of public health has been forgotten among the experts who should best understand this. Is it possible that sociology is actually a necessary science in the current period?

2

Isolation. What is social "isolation"—distancing, quarantine? A paradox: isolation is an irreducibly collective phenomenon. This is so in two senses. First, isolation depends on a vast network of cooperative labor that makes it possible. Goods continue to arrive at our door produced in fields and factories, packaged in warehouses, shelved in grocery stores, and delivered finally via smartphone-connected drivers and the postal service. Only this collective work allows us to "isolate." Isolation is thus both an expression of the division of social labor and a class and racial phenomenon resting on specific material conditions: sufficient resources, security of income, independence of work. No room for moralism here.

There is also an experiential dimension to "collective isolation." To be isolated among other isolating persons is an entirely different experience to that of being isolated among persons who are not isolated. Isolation is not the state of being alone. To isolate is to participate in an experience that is completely common. I feel paradoxically more connected to friends, family, loved ones even through the mediation of technology. (But is technology really so decisive? Certainly video chats are nice, allowing for the recreation in cyber-space of a whole social life. But if we had only telephones, or the mail, would it be that different?) To be isolated when others were connected would be horrible. This is a different kind of experience. Isolation is a form of group behavior; to be isolated is to be part of a collectivity. Could there a politics of isolation?

Isolation is also an expression of community, and care for the community. "The best thing you can do for your country is stay home." So enjoins the liberal press. Thus, an inversion. Sociability becomes an expression of pathological individualism, heedlessness, egocentrism. Isolation becomes a patriotic duty. (But too often its material preconditions are denied.)

3

Friends and enemies. The polling is clear: Trump is benefiting politically from the coronavirus.* His approval rating has increased five points nationally from January, and this is not just among Republicans. His approval rating among Democrats has increased from 7 to 12 percent. Among core Democratic voting blocs (African Americans and Latinos) his approval has increased about 10 percent (8 to 18 percent, and 27 to 37 percent, respectively). It is urgent to understand why.

The first point to keep in mind is that catastrophic mistakes resulting in millions of deaths have often redounded to the political benefit of their perpetrators. Did Hitler suffer in popularity from his invasion of the USSR? Probably not. Even though he did not appear again in public after Stalingrad, the German population fought to the bitter end. Did Stalin suffer from the Holodomor? Hard to say, given the meaninglessness of "public opinion" in the USSR

---

* Pew Research Center, "Worries about Coronavirus Surge, as Most Americans Expect a Recession—or Worse," March 26, 2020.

of the 1930s, but millions of Soviet citizens rallied to him
in the Great Patriotic War. Did Emperor Hirohito suffer
politically from the monumentally idiotic attack on Pearl
Harbor? If anything, the opposite is the case. The conclusion: if Trump, as seems probable, becomes responsible for
tens of thousands of his fellow citizens' deaths, there is every
reason to believe that this may aid him not for logical but
for political reasons.

What is the mechanism at work here? It is what the
German political theorist Carl Schmitt called "the political": the opposition between "friend" and "enemy." Trump
instinctively understands that this distinction is the real
basis of his political appeal. He never falls for the liberal
illusion that politics is a "talking shop" or a matter of
solving technical problems. He "understands," if it can be
called that, that "the political" supersedes distinctions such
as competence/incompetence, good/evil, truth/falsehood. He
always returns to this basic opposition. This helps him in an
obvious, and a not-so-obvious, way. First, it helps him with
his base: he can always present attacks on his competence,
his truthfulness, or his goodness as political. And he is right.

But there is a not-so-obvious way that this constant
return to the political aids Trump; for the virus, by common
consent, is also an "enemy." Thus, Trump benefits both from
a rallying of his base and a rallying to the flag: thus, his
improving position in the polls. It is useless to decry the
electorate. The first thing to understand, and to make understood, is that Trump is not most relevantly an incompetent,
evil liar. He is, most relevantly, an enemy.

4

Politics in command. What is the nature of the political
economy emerging from the coronavirus? Are we heading
toward "state capitalism," or "neofeudalism," or something

altogether different? To begin to answer this question it is first necessary to understand the character of the crisis. One, quite common, framing interprets the coronavirus as an exogenous shock to an otherwise healthy economy. Even the perceptive editorial by Saez and Zucman in the *New York Times* contains a version of this idea. The authors write, "The firms seeking aid today bear no direct responsibility for the disaster that threatens their survival."* It should be emphasized, though, that although the coronavirus in one sense is exogenous, it intersects with an already extremely fragile economy.

First, it is crucial to understand the long-term shift in the American economy since the early 1980s away from a model of "retain and reinvest," in which corporations used profits to invest in plants and equipment, thereby expanding productivity and employment, to a model of "downsize and distribute" in which corporations did not invest, but rather prioritized shareholder value and redistributed profits. A more recent phenomenon is the explosion of corporate debt. As a group of *Financial Times* journalists put it, "Companies have gorged on cheap debt for over a decade, sending the global outstanding stock of nonfinancial corporate bonds to an all-time high of 13.5 trillion dollars by the end of last year." This level of corporate indebtedness is "double where it stood in December 2008 in real terms."† The debt binge has been made possible by the enormous expansion of liquidity and historically low interest rates engineered by central banks over the years since the 2008 financial crisis. According to the *FT*, a huge tranche of corporate junk bonds, which are basically loans made to very unprofitable firms, are coming due over the next five years.

---

* Emmanuel Saez and Gabriel Zucman, "Jobs Aren't Being Destroyed This Fast Elsewhere. Why Is That?," *New York Times*, March 30, 2020.

† Andrew Edgecliffe-Johnson, et al., "Will the Coronavirus Trigger a Corporate Debt Crisis?," *Financial Times*, March 12, 2020.

The coronavirus crisis has exposed this crisis; it has not created it.

A major question is, Why have investors been so willing to purchase double-B- and triple-C-rated corporate bonds? The answer: there are no obvious alternatives. The long-standing crisis of profitability in the real economy explains the lack of investment there, and the turn toward more and more dubious sources of returns. Again, this crisis preexists the coronavirus, although the coronavirus has certainly revealed and compounded it.

The second point is that the CARES Act's largest single budget item is a massive $500 billion slush fund to be administered by the Secretary of the Treasury with little other than symbolic oversight. The $350 billion support to small businesses is organized in a different way. The funds will be funneled through the Small Business Administration, and from there to banks, who will then pass them on to borrowers while collecting fees. The loans will be entirely forgiven if they are used to retain personnel; if small businesses break the terms, the funds will be converted into ultra-low-interest loans. Both packages, however, suggest the emergence of a new political economy: one where "politics is in command." The CARES Act continues the now venerable tradition of massive handouts to large corporations, of which TARP and the Affordable Care Act are two further examples. It extends those handouts to smaller businesses with banks as the intermediaries. But what has become ever more obvious since 2008 is a reconfiguration of the whole relationship between politics and economics. What determines rates of return in the new political economy is not one's ability to compete on price against other firms in a market, but rather one's access to political authority.

What about successful firms like Amazon, or the various cloud services that are likely to do well out of the crisis? These firms increasingly derive their profits from their monopolistic or monopsonistic position in markets, which, although initially gained through competitive struggle, tends to be reproduced by political means.

These are very dangerous developments. The increasing importance of political power as a determinant of the rate of return is one of the basic reasons for the hollowing out of democracy. But viewed more dialectically, socialism is now increasingly a reality. Market power and political power tend to fuse. The question is not whether political authority will massively intervene to determine the overall pattern of investment and the distribution of income; the question is whether this authority will be subject to democratic control or will devolve in an authoritarian direction.

5

Allocation. The distribution of medical supplies in response to the coronavirus is a classic economic problem: the "allocation of scarce resources." The same thing is true of the distribution of aid in the CARES legislation recently passed by Congress. The Trump administration has been widely attacked for the handling of these two economic problems, especially of the first one. Why is that? Basically, the objection comes down to this: in an emergency, prices do not function efficiently. What is needed instead is a "federally coordinated response"; that is, economic planning. But the Trump administration could rightly respond, "Since when are markets supposed to be inefficient?" If there were anyone in the White House who had bothered to read Hayek, they could cite him to the effect that a "competitive market order" generates "greater knowledge and wealth than could ever be obtained or utilized in a centrally directed economy." On Hayekian grounds—that is to say on the intellectual terrain that has defined virtually every administration since the Reagan revolution—the competition among states for ventilators, denounced as "like being on eBay with 50 other states" by Andrew Cuomo, would be completely correct. This is a market functioning to allocate scarce resources. The prices it produces express the revealed preferences of the governors.

It may be worth articulating the intellectual basis of Cuomo's thought that this market is absurd. Cuomo himself of course resists any broader conclusion and appeals to pure pragmatism. (It's interesting that whenever he discusses this issue, he is careful to eschew "concepts," insisting that his proposals are driven purely by exigencies.) But it is not true that federal planning in the distribution of ventilators is obviously superior to prices. The rationale for why planning is superior needs to be explained.

The reason the market is inefficient in this case is that the good we are after is fundamentally collective: the good being pursued here is public health, and in fact ultimately the health of the entire population of the world. (There is an unattractive and retrograde nationalism that often creeps into critiques of the system. "How can we let this happen in this country?" As if to say, it would be just fine for it to happen in Thailand, India, or Kenya. The virus is now in every one of the fifty-four African countries, and promises to become an unimaginable catastrophe on that continent and elsewhere in the developing world.) To distribute medical supplies according to market logic assumes that the health of one state, or even one country or region, can be achieved while that of other states, countries, or regions can be allowed to deteriorate. But this is the central fallacy of the market operating here. The allocation of resources to any unit other than the public, and at the limit the world public, as a whole, undermines the utility or use value of the commodity being allocated. To allow an outbreak anywhere is to allow an outbreak everywhere. The only rational allocation of resources under these conditions is according to medically determined requirements of suppressing the outbreak. And this requires an allocation not according to prices, but according to scientific knowledge about where the outbreak is most severe. (Here the consistency of the Trump administration is, in a way, admirable. The absence of testing creates an absence of knowledge in which market prices are left as the only possible basis of allocation. Hayek's own celebration of blind processes ought to be recalled at this point.)

An important question is how broadly this logic should extend. Surely there are many goods like this. Natural spaces, the global weather system, education. Obviously, the allocation of a national park or wilderness area undermines its use. It can only maintain that use on the condition that that it is appropriated collectively. The same is true clearly of climate change. If we think of a stable global weather system as a good, it is only a good if it is a collective good. Similarly, what use is education in a sea of ignorance? That's why it is so urgent not to let the argument for federal coordination be made on merely pragmatic grounds. The economic problem posed by the coronavirus would best be solved within the framework of collectivism.

6

Founding fathers. Discussion of "coronavirus bonds," an instrument of debt mutualization intended to aid the ailing economies especially of Spain and Italy, prompts reflection on the problem of Europe. European debt politics are as follows. The leaders of the southern European countries want to mutualize their debt by creating instruments backed by a mix of low-interest-rate German and Dutch bonds and high-interest-rate Italian and Spanish ones. Dutch and German leadership resists this argument, claiming that this would put hardworking Nordic taxpayers on the hook for debts incurred by their irresponsible southern neighbors. The Mediterraneans counterargue that Europe must be governed by principles of solidarity, and subtly remind the Germans that they paid no reparations at the end of World War II. The result is predictable: fuel to the fire of the far right, the latest Italian iteration of which is the new political party Fratelli d'Italia (drawing its name from the first stanza of the national anthem).

There is obfuscation on both sides of the debate. To be clear, no one is advocating bailing out the Italian and Spanish populations. The debate is actually quite narrowly about who should bail out bondholders. "Solidarity" in this framework means all Europeans should pull together to make bondholders whole, while the Nordic option asserts that the burden should be shifted onto those populations who are least able to pay. This is a miserable choice. Is there another option? Of course, it's called "debt repudiation." Only such a policy would create solidarity among European peoples based on their common interests as debtors.

There is a striking similarity between these politics and those of the early American Republic with its opposition between Federalist or Hamiltonian bondholders and Democratic or Jeffersonian debtors. In the United States the debate was solved by the victory of the Federalists. The prospects for the European Hamiltonians look bright as well. Is it possible, however, to imagine a "neo-Jeffersonian" Europe? Probably only when the current structure is thrown onto the scrapheap of history where its response to the pandemic, among so many other cataclysmic failures, indicates it richly deserves to be. What might emerge from that is a United States of Europe that is much more democratic than the oligarchic republic that consolidated on the shores of the western Atlantic in the late eighteenth century.

7

Walking. Hegel taught that in the modern state one comes to recognize oneself as a citizen by recognizing the citizenship of all others in the political community. Citizenship is thus a mirror structure of mutual recognition. The coronavirus, however, imposes a new structure of recognition. The phenomenon is evident even in the most mundane activity: taking a walk. Walkers, whether in small cohabiting groups or as individuals, carefully maintain distance by orienting to all other walkers. If their paths could be traced, they would form an elaborate network of braids as streets are crossed and crossed again. But what structure of recognition is this that produces the ambulatory distancing of a walk in the age of the coronavirus?

First, it certainly is a structure of recognition. The walkers are much more attentive to each other than would normally be the case. The absent-minded solitary walker of the pre-virus age is nowhere to be found. These are walkers whose dispersion is mutually coordinated by a sustained collective effort. But what does each walker or group of walkers see in all the other walkers? Simply this: the threat of death. Every walker is a potential vector of disease. But, in homology to the mirror structure of citizenship, by seeing others as a vector each walker sees herself as a vector. Mutual recognition here is not the mutual recognition of a political status, but a biological one. As such it is also universal. The consequence: the virus, by underlining this common status, also makes absurd all institutions that would confine, restrict movement, or force contact. The prison, the border, the assembly line, the Amazon warehouse—how can any of these be justified in an age that forces us to face the human condition: virus incubator?

8

Night watchman. What sort of threat does Trump pose to the state? One answer suggests that Trump and his administration embody an "antigovernment" ideology. The suggestion is that the present administration is a radical form of liberalism or neoliberalism.

Actually, there is an important difference between Trump and neoliberalism. One can be a champion of "limited government" while embracing a technocratic conception of the state. Neoliberals, after all, love independent central banks. Indeed, the project of neoliberalism is as much about strengthening the state's technocratic core as it is limiting the scope of its actions.

With the Trump administration, a new conception of rule emerges. Max Weber identified both the objective and the subjective dimensions of the bureaucracy as "the office."* Objectively, the office requires:

(a) separation of office from household;
(b) separation of spheres of competence;
(c) special expert training;
(d) career;
(e) money salary; and
(f) written files.

Subjectively, the office only requires one thing: that office-holding be oriented to as an impersonal calling (the Calvinist coloring is obvious here). An official in the "pure type" acts on the basis of duty to an objective order that transcends his or her personal interests.

---

* Max Weber, *Economy and Society: An Outline of Interpretive Sociology, Vol.* 2 (Berkeley, Los Angeles, and London: University of California Press, 1978), pp. 956–63.

It is difficult to overstate the degree to which the Trump administration attacks every dimension of "office" in this sense. Instead of separation of household and office, a blending of them; instead of separation of spheres of competence, the emergence of questionably competent plenipotentiaries (Jared Kushner, for instance). Instead of special expert training, a cult of incompetence. Instead of careerism, amateurism. Instead of money salary, massive corruption; and instead of written files, a deep hostility to all records.

In the context of the coronavirus this has emerged in a particularly clear form in the debate over the distribution of ventilators and personal protective equipment, or PPE. Kushner's revealing comment was that this equipment is "ours," not the "state's." The "ours" clearly referred to the persons in the administration and revealed that neither he, nor Trump, nor the other members of the administration understand themselves as occupying offices. The idea of objective order is anathema to them.

But what is the meaning of this mutation of office into something like "table companion"? The idea of the state as an objective order is certainly not a mere description; it is also a central feature of the ideology of the capitalist state. It is not the person or the class that rules, but the subject-less order. The state is a pure parameter, framework, or guarantor for the social processes that play out within it, much in the way that a bell jar full of gas is a parameter for the molecules that fly about inside it.

Thus, should Trump be seen in one way as unmasking the fiction of the impersonal state, of the state as *veilleur de nuit*?

What sorts of political opportunities does the Trumpian attack on "office" open for those seeking a more just world? If the state is obviously no longer an objective order but a tool at the service of interests, the project must not be to restore its phantom objectivity, but to orient the state in a new way. What is needed today is a new pact, a new charter, an oriented constitution that stipulates a goal, direction, or telos for the political order. The choice is no longer between the state as a procedural order and what Victor Pérez-Díaz called the state as the "bearer of a moral project." The choice is between the state as the "bearer of an immoral project" and the state as the bearer of a moral one.

The figure of the new state cannot, however, be the bureaucrat; it must be the cadre, the omnicompetent figure who relativizes all procedures in relation to the substantive cause that animates her action: today in the struggle against the virus, whose primary figure is the female nurse with improvised protective equipment, tomorrow in the struggle for a new order that will require analogous competencies. The days of the formal state and the spontaneous order are over. The dawn of comradeship, of cadre, of collective struggle is breaking in the hospitals, in the nursing homes, in the clinics. Could there be a new type of soviet, analogous to the soviets of workers, soldiers, and peasants in the Russian Revolution? Imagine the soviet of nurses, homecare workers, and nursing home assistants. But does the struggle against the virus create the cadre and comrade as the struggle in the trenches did?

9

Soma. Can health care be a commodity? In the United States, every "service" has its price. Conceptually, the provision of health care in this system is thought of in the same way that the cafeteria restaurants that used to be popular in the 1970s priced and delivered food. (I still remember fondly the slightly pasty taste of "Blue Boar" mashed potatoes, whose flavor could never be reproduced at home with an actual tuber.) In any case the doctor is conceptually a "server" who offers the "client" a particular item. The sovereign patient/consumer can then choose among the options: Would you like to have a side of nursing with your chemotherapy? It's always nice to round out your treatment with an extra helping of nutritionist advice. We have two different courses of treatment that you can follow: you are free to choose, just as you are free to choose the chicken, steak, or fish at the cafeteria. But, of course, the commodity form is entirely inappropriate to the "service" on offer: health. Why is this so?

The first problem is that the "patient/consumer" is fundamentally ignorant and stands in a relationship of layperson to expert in the context of health care. This is all obscured by the falsely demotic language of "empowerment" that enjoins the patient to "take charge" of her own care. But the entire reason that the patient seeks care is that doctors, nurses, and specialists are experts: they are not offering "services." Instead, they are presumably in a position to determine which "services" have an actual use for the patient. But the commodity form undermines the expert/patient relationship by establishing a false sovereignty for the patients. (Inevitably this is reinforced by the ubiquitous customer satisfaction survey. "Did you enjoy your surgical experience?") The sprawling apparatus of US health care is premised on the fiction of the patient as a sovereign consumer: the reality is anxiety and bewilderment.

The second problem posed by the commodity form is that health "services" violate the concept of marginal utility. There is no reason to think that the "utility" of an additional unit of health care will eventually decline as the number of total units of health care consumed increases. This is because "utility" here is not a quantitative accumulation, but a qualitative state: health. This state cannot be reduced to any series of fungible units, which is why, by the way, the saying "health is wealth" is absolutely false. The third problem is that health care provision cannot be described by an indifference curve in which one commodity can be swapped out for another: two open-heart surgeries and an appendectomy cannot be substituted with a kidney transplant and cataract removal. The reason is that health care makes sense only in relationship to a specific illness and is meant to restore its recipient to a specific state.

10

Neoliberal nightmares. Hayek's greatest fear, and the thing that set him apart so clearly from his classical forebears like Smith, was that socialism might be the default condition of humanity. It is this gnawing sensation that drove his obsessive defense of the price mechanism and its various moral and institutional supports. If he was right, perhaps the massive historicizing apparatus of Marxism has misled to some extent. For crises (social or personal) reveal an extensive network of reciprocity resting just under the surface of capitalist society. The proof of its existence lies simply in the fact that hundreds of millions of people have not been thrown into the street: the social mechanism still works. How is this it all possible? Socialism is already here; it needs only a crisis to reveal it. Or perhaps this is just the idle dream that emerges every time the humanized society recedes beyond the horizon of the attainable. Anarchists and opportunists are forever forgetting politics; they are most appealing when politics itself seems hopeless.

11

Where to stand? Standpoints are again a topic. But in the discussion about them certain basic confusions seem always to reemerge that lead to cul-de-sacs at once political and intellectual. First point: the mode in which agents regard the social world, whether in the stance of onlooking or in the stance of active participation, is at least as significant as the perspective from which one sees it. Lukács understood this, and Bourdieu either rediscovered or plagiarized the idea. (It is never clear with him, as his work consists mostly in more or less felicitous rediscoveries and plagiarisms.)

Second point: to say that a certain standpoint provides more adequate access to the real is not a social-psychological hypothesis; it is an epistemological one. Again, Lukács saw this most clearly. His argument is a bit of elegant Kantian-esque bootstrapping. It goes roughly like this: Marxism exists as scientific knowledge of history, and as a revolutionary practice. Hence, there must be some standpoint from which that knowledge and that sort of practice is possible. (Note the parallel between Marx/Newton and Lukács/Kant. Lukács is Marx's Kant.) That standpoint is the proletariat, a subject that in order to act as a subject must have an adequate understanding both of its own nature and of the historical process. (This is not true of the bourgeoisie; it is an interesting question why.)

The key point in this series is not that manual workers have socially conditioned insight into the real workings of capitalism and its tendencies, but that in order for manual workers to act as a subject of history they must also under-stand the real nature of capitalism. This is the meaning of the common slogan "It is not a matter of what the working class thinks, but rather of what it is." It is important to insist on this point in the context of what Olúfémi Táíwò calls "deference epistemology," the notion that certain persons because of their identities have an immediate access to ade-quate knowledge and should therefore be "deferred to."*
Experience becomes knowledge only through mediation, as the given comes to be understood in a larger context and through different lenses, as it were. What is meant by "standpoint" is the position from which this process of

---

* Olúfémi O. Táíwò, "Being in the Room Privilege: Elite Capture and Epistemic Deference," *The Philosopher* 8, no. 4, December 2020.

mediation unfolds. It can never be reduced to a privileged experience because it is also the transcendence and relativization of experience, although experience should never, for that reason, be forgotten.

12

The rich. Bumper stickers sometimes encapsulate the whole political situation. Sighted yesterday in the Oakland hills: "Tax the Ultra-Rich" stuck on a late-model Audi SUV. The sponsor was the Warren campaign. The extreme dispersion of wealth and income at the very top of the distribution leads to this sort of thing. Thus not: "Tax the Rich," or even "Tax the Very Rich," but "Tax the Ultra-Rich." "Ultra-Rich"? Presumably the category does not include Audi owners who live in the Oakland hills. The slogan exemplifies the weakness of American "progressivism"; its social coalition is heavily based on an upper middle class that one must assume is more than supportive of taxes on the "ultras," but would have little interest in shouldering any greater burdens itself. The political coalition of the current Democratic Party depends on generating just enough fiscal revenue to hold the bottom of the alliance while never overstepping the bounds of the top. "Ultra" shows the upper limit clearly.

13

Reactionaries. Democracy's reactionary critics are as a rule far more perceptive about representative regimes than liberal apologists. Men like Mosca, or Schmitt, or Weber see the key weakness of these regimes: the ambiguous notion of representation. The point is that in a regime of popular sovereignty the people cannot be represented (unless with short, revocable mandates). These considerations are directly applicable to the current moment. There are many misleading analogies made between Trump and interwar fascism. But one important actual similarity is ignored. Neither the interwar fascists nor Trump can be described as antidemocratic in the sense that they reject the will of the demos; they claim in fact to embody it. What they do oppose is the current regime of representation. This is what constantly wrong-foots the liberals, who end up arguing that existing arrangements of whatever sort are democratic, and that Trump is antidemocratic because he attacks these—or damages "norms," or whatever. The absurdity is evident. The federal courts democratic? They were established as a counterweight to democracy. The Senate democratic? Not even in theory, since it represents the states, not the people. The FBI? The CIA? To pose the question is to answer it. Trump's claim is that he represents the people against this corrupt regime. How is that antidemocratic?

14

Uncle Joe. The historical analogies that a culture selects to understand its political present are revealing. The Trump/fascism comparison offers a kind of generic signifier for political evil. Interestingly, though, he is rarely paired with specific political figures of the radical right. Hitler comparisons are somehow beyond the pale, and Mussolini, because of the disdainful ignorance that most of the chattering classes display toward Italian history, is seen as a comic figure. In contrast, there is one man of the left with whom Trump is regularly linked: Stalin. The oddity and irrelevance of this pairing aside, it serves an important purpose: to invoke the ghost of totalitarianism, salve to the liberal intelligentsia.

15

Critique. Why does sociology lack a culture of critique? Undoubtedly, the sociology of knowledge, especially in its Bourdieusian form, bears a heavy responsibility. The basic task of the critic is to deal with the text before him or her. The piece must be treated in the first instance as a self-standing structure, like a built object (although it must also be subsequently contextualized historically). It should not be dissolved in the acid bath of "positionality," or alternatively treated as the expression of a stance in the field. One effect of approaching culture from the perspective of a reduction to biography or of stance-taking is that it becomes impossible to treat ideas seriously; and as a result, critique also becomes impossible, or rather a suspect activity. The critic, after all, also has a position in a field, an agenda, etc., so why bother with what he or she says? Reviews, in this context, become more or less sincere advertisements.

16

Futures past. Two caesuras divided last year between a before and after by what seems like an unbridgeable chasm. The first occurred on March 11, 2020, the day before my wife's birthday, when we made the final decision to depart for Napa and Covid began for our family. The second was on August 24, when we were shaken by devastating medical news. The very recent past feels both very near and unattainably far. The past of normal routine, of driving to lessons, track meets, university, etc., is gone. Most painfully gone is the future of that past. What lies in store? This gnaws at me incessantly. It is no longer contained within the horizon of a project. The advice I've gotten, which seems sensible, is to live in the present—to orient to time in a new way. But the problem is that the future is so much a part of what the present or the now is that it is impossible to follow the advice.

17

Time. How does historical time progress? The sense I described in the last note, of the loss of a future-past, is also relevant on the historical scale. For what was lost in 1991 was not "really existing human emancipation," but rather human emancipation as a possible future. The key question on the historic plane, as it was on the personal plane, is how to avoid nostalgia—the melancholy longing for a situation that no longer exists. The most reasonable proposal seems to be this: Imagine a vast articulated tree. One can move along the tree in one direction only: thus, no going back. At any given moment one is faced with a determinant set of paths: either a, or b, or c. These are highly constrained. (That is what is normally called "structure.") Agency consists in the capacity to choose among the paths. (There are further details to be considered. For example, the number of paths may be either expanded or contracted by the cognitive and imaginative capacity of the agent at particular points. Thus, in a sense these capacities too are part of the structure.) The project of human emancipation—if we now imagine humanity on that tree—consists at this moment in "choosing" the paths that could make human emancipation a possible future once again. To put it idiomatically, it is a matter of "getting on the right track."

18

Petite bourgeoisie. Among the many economic processes currently unfolding, one seems particularly important: the agony of the petite bourgeoisie. My son and I had an interesting conversation with an ethnically Tibetan shop owner. He bemoaned the corruption behind how government assistance is being doled out through the "Paycheck Protection Program." He had tried to apply for a loan, but his bank could not even explain how to fill out the forms. He also denounced, however, the inconstancy of California's stay-at-home orders. He described a restaurant owner friend of his who had spent thousands of dollars to build outdoor tables and purchase heaters; the investment was a total loss, as the restaurant had been forced to close again entirely after a few days of being open. Clearly, the politics of this group, small-scale shop and restaurant owners, will be crucial in the coming period. The petite bourgeoisie feels squeezed between the connected fat cats served by the federal government and public health measures that threaten its economic survival. Great political intelligence will be needed to avoid its radicalization to the right.

19

The Capitol. The "insurrection" of three days ago (I write this on January 9) has unleashed among other things a "classification struggle." Are the participants "terrorists," "protesters," "patriots," a "mob"? These are not only descriptors, but also weapons in the political struggle. What can be said about this beyond the oversaturated media discussion that has ensued? The observations that follow are largely based on a thirty-minute video, made by one of the participants, that is a kind of instant historical document. It might be useful to begin with an encapsulation of the description emerging from the mainstream press. It says, roughly, that the "mob" was composed of white supremacists intent on overthrowing democracy. As evidence, journalists point to the presence of neo-Nazis and confederate nostalgists in the crowd, as well as its overwhelmingly white makeup.

But there are problems with this description. Surprisingly, the crowd contained a few people of color; it was not homogenously white. More importantly, the basic demand of the "insurrectionists" was that a stolen election be made right. This was coupled with the claim that the Capitol is "ours." As far as I could tell—and perhaps more evidence would qualify this judgment—explicitly white-supremacist demands were unusual. What to make of all this? The point is that in their own view the insurrectionists were small "d" democrats acting as Jeffersonian tyrant slayers. They viewed the Capitol as an iniquitous den of corruption. Were they wrong?

A further point that the media has raised, and that Biden has even adopted, is the comparison between the treatment of these protesters and that of the Black Lives Matter activists at Lafayette Square over the summer. Celebrities and media personalities have rightly drawn attention to the difference between the attitude of the police toward the extremely racially diverse crowds of the summer and that toward the mostly white and older crowd at the Capitol. The conclusion, drawn by most, is that the attitude of the police is also a manifestation of white supremacy. But a more careful account is needed here. The *forze dell'ordine* never treat left and right protesters symmetrically. This is because the police represent, among other things, a specific crystallization of class power; they are not a third party standing above the fray. Leftists or progressives should be clear-eyed about this rather than feigning outrage and surprise.

More concretely, the crowds that invaded the Capitol

were clearly sociologically closer to some of the police than were the BLM protesters: racially, occupationally, educationally. That proximity also found expression in the symbology of the insurrectionists: chants of "U-S-A!," dozens of variously embellished American flags, the Jeffersonian flag, together with a smattering of Confederate battle flags and crypto–national socialist symbols. These, in other words, were mostly (except for the last) the banal decorative paraphernalia of US nationalism. Such symbols, which clearly have the effect of mentally disarming the police, could never become the dominant motifs of a BLM protest. A final thought that few have remarked upon, but which is obvious from listening to what the crowd actually said: among the "insurrectionists," the most common definition of the enemy was "socialism," sometimes mixed with "communism" and "Marxism." This, however, only shows their lack of originality, since condemnation of the socialist tradition is shared across the entire political and intellectual spectrum.

20

Jeffersonians. Is there a rational core to the antisocialism described in note 19? Certainly, a revolt against socialism is an oddity in a country with such a minuscule and powerless left. But what do the Trumpists actually mean by "socialism"? Socialism, in their minds, is associated with corruption: the illegitimate transfer of resources from their legitimate producers to variously specified parasites. (The Squad, for example, is constantly condemned as both radical and corrupt.) In that sense Trumpism can be summarized as a reactionary revolt against "political capitalism," however much it also embodies it. Its dream is the Jeffersonian petit bourgeois utopia of self-made men without the welfare state, financiers, and paper money. As American, as they say, as apple pie.

21

Truth. Timothy Snyder's rise to prominence is one of the clearest symptoms of the putrescence of the liberal intelligentsia in the age of Trump. What is Snyder's message? That shared "truths" are the foundation of democracy, and that what undermines democracy is lying. There are two main difficulties with Snyder's view. Lies, euphemisms, and hypocrisy are the lifeblood of US politics. Furthermore, what really distinguishes Trump is not that he lies, even though he does that very often, but that he sometimes spectacularly tells the truth. One of his truest speeches came immediately after the 2020 election when he accused Biden, Schumer, and Pelosi of being creatures of high finance and Wall Street. Or recall when he skewered Jeb Bush in a debate before the South Carolina primary by reminding the audience of the Iraq debacle. Perhaps what Snyder meant to say is that the basis of democracy is the elite's shared commitment to patriotic hypocrisy, a commitment that Trump did not share since his only value appeared to be self-enrichment. Is it too much to think this might have a salutary effect?

22

The center. Italian history is an inexhaustible storehouse of examples and analogies broadly applicable to the politics of capitalist societies. One that may be useful in the coming period is *centrismo*: the complex coalitional politics of the Democrazia Cristiana (DC) in the period after 1948 when the communists had been definitively excluded from a governing role at the national level. Italy consolidated in these decades, up until 1976, as a frozen republic. Although elections occurred, only one party was able to hold national power (the DC). The entire structure was oriented to keeping the communist party out of power, since it was considered both by the Italian political elite and perhaps more importantly the Americans to be unsuited to governing. The events of January 6 in the United States may open up an opportunity for the Democratic Party in the United States to carry out an analogous policy vis-à-vis the Republicans. What would this look like?

The Democrats would consolidate as a vast coalition stretching from the Democratic Socialists of America to Lincoln Project Republicans. The currents would be held together by the relatively thin program of "multiracial democracy" offered as an alternative to the MAGA crowd. The radicalized rump of the Republican Party would run its red strongholds in the Plains states and the upper South virtually without opposition at the local level: an inverted analogue to "Red Emilia." (The Deep South, the old Cotton Belt, is shifting rapidly; it will likely not be a Republican stronghold for much longer.) The economic center of gravity of the Democratic Party would shift further to the right as it vote-hunts in the affluent suburbs with ever greater success. The upshot of *centrismo all'americana* would be to greatly diminish the electoral prospects of the Republicans and at the same time to chloroform the young DSA left. But there is a problem. The DC's coalitional success was ultimately based on the "Economic Miracle" of the postwar years. Biden comes to power amid a distributional struggle of ferocious intensity and slow growth. There is also a personal difference: Scranton Joe is no Alcide De Gasperi.

23

Class. The debate about whether class or race is the most important factor in understanding US politics drags on with little clarity or apparent resolution. On the side of the neo-Kautskyites we hear the claim that an appeal to the economic interests of workers (rarely ever conceptually specified) will win out in every case over cultural appeals to whiteness. Unfortunately, say these adherents, the Democratic Party, either because of its stupidity or its cravenness, never sufficiently makes this appeal and therefore repeatedly sabotages its electoral prospects. On the other side we hear that American politics has always been "about race," and that the American right in particular is based on an appeal to white supremacy. Each side in the struggle has its social science: the academic studies that purport to show that either class or race is the key to understanding the Trump electoral base in particular.

But what are classes? What are races? These basic conceptual issues are left in the cognitive mire of everyday political jargon. Classes are usually identified with something economic, and ultimately are identified with income groups. (Thus, the observation, common among progressives, that Trump voters have a higher average income than their Democratic counterparts and thus Trumpism cannot have a working-class base; this is based on the confusion of class position with income, so that, for example, young professionals can appear more "working class" than middle-aged manufacturing workers.) Races, in contrast, have something to do with culture and identity.

But both of these are inadequate formulations. Class as the underlying magnetic field of politics can be organized at the level of civil society, the "first level of the superstructure," as Gramsci would say, in different ways. Two are of particular significance. Class struggle can be organized as struggles among coalitions of market positions; coalitions which will have a strong tendency to consolidate as "races"—for example, northern workers and capitalists in the late nineteenth-century US who came together as a nativist white bloc against competition from foreign goods and foreign persons—but can also take other forms such as religious affinity (as in the DC coalition in

Italy), or national or regional identity. Or class struggle can be organized as a conflict between antagonistic positions in relations of exploitation. One important conclusion is that race—far from being an alternative to class, or a cross-cutting "dimension"—is a possible, indeed probable, way in which the class struggle comes to be organized at the level of civil society.

As is always the case in debates of this sort, the correct formulation must break with the immediacy of the terms in which the discussion is posed. Thus, if it is found that racial identity explains an aspect of politics, the further question must always be, "Why would the class struggle take the form of a struggle among races over this particular issue, and at this particular time, and in this particular place in history?" Conversely, if the class struggle takes the form of a struggle among groups locked in antagonistic relations of exploitation at the level of civil society, this too must be explained. It is, after all, only a possible, and perhaps unlikely organization of the class struggle. In any case, it is always a matter of treating the given structure of political conflict as a form of appearance. This is why class analysis can never be reduced to a substantive explanation; it is also always a methodological position: one that holds that reality is never exhausted by the given.

24

Reducing. What is reductionism? The accusation that an analysis is reductionist usually refers to the attempt to explain some feature of politics with reference to economic interests. But this is both imprecise and not general enough to capture the problem. The concept of reductionism should be replaced with the concept of "immediacy." Perhaps the phrase "immediatism" could be used. This is something similar to what Antonio Labriola called the "theory of historical factors": the idea that political or social outcomes are produced by one or more factors or givens that cause them. The point is not to deny causality, but to demand that it be conceptually mediated: in other words, that the conditions under which the causal relations hold be specified.

25

Beauty/pain. It might be thought that the sheer physical beauty of the place with its stunning sunsets in which the light drips down the hills like liquid gold, with its eerily blue sky, and with its breath-stealing ocean views would make things easier to bear; instead, it feels like nature itself is mocking our pain.

26

Sociology. For Parsonians or modernization theorists more generally—a category that in relationship to this question includes the vast majority of sociologists—sociology has replaced Marxism much as science replaces religion in Comte's scheme. For neo-Marxism following Lukács's lead in *The Destruction of Reason*, sociology is rather a reaction to Marxism: a totalizing counterscience provoked by the theory of its class enemy. Burawoy's suggestion in this connection is interesting: sociology should somehow be seen as fitting inside Marxism. But the thesis requires elaboration. Marxism is fundamentally an account of the succession of modes of production with particular emphasis on capitalism. Its sociology though is rather an afterthought. Classes and their struggles are important primarily because they provide a mechanism of revolution. But the relationship of "phenomenal" human groups to the basic places determined by the fundamental patterns of exploitation in society is extraordinarily difficult to specify.

Marx's statements about the simplification of the class struggle with the development of capitalism could not be more misleading. It was Gramsci who saw the basic issue most clearly. The development of capitalism did not lead to the appearance of classes at the level of politics. Rather there emerged a whole new massive "superstructural" level, which constituted a plane of immediate experience made up of a whirling kaleidoscope of groups. The reality of class now receded behind this screen of false pluralism that constituted the phenomenal world of the social. (It should always be remembered that Gramsci is a specifically post-Bernsteinian and post-Sorelian thinker.) The task of politics is in the first place to reorganize this experiential/political world as a world of classes: to make the "noumenal" realm of the structure converge with the "phenomenal" realm of civil society. What then is the place of sociology, and in what sense does it sit inside Marxism? Its task is the study of civil society as a particular configuration or form of appearance of the basic structural positions in the exploitation relations of capitalism.

27

The South. I remember the weirdly wholesome smell of curing tobacco in the old barn where the sunlight slid in through gaps in the boards, half illuminating the leaves hanging from the rafters. Silent and with high vaulted ceilings like the cathedral at Chartres, and holy like that as well. I remember that brown syrupy sweet drink with tangy lemon that Mamaw called "sweet tea." I remember Ransom, wild and free and laughing, who encouraged me, so family lore says, to eat a raw onion freshly pulled from the ground, which is why I don't like onions anymore. Some years later, after we moved to Louisville from the Maddoxes' farm, I remember the pasty countenance of the man picking up his daughter—she loathed him—from my grade school. It was early in the age of Reagan, and at this time one could tell a politician, or a banker, or an insurance salesman by this sartorial sign: the jackass pants, an ill-fitting khaki exemplifying complacency and greed. The man was Mitch McConnell, that very type of mediocre white-collar dad, although his ugly shirts were usually blue if memory serves; we all felt very badly for Elly to be saddled with such a parent. Hard to imagine a figure more out of place on the Maddox farm; and yet, they almost certainly voted for him: their opposite in every way. That's the conundrum of much of the rural politics of the United States. We could put it this way: When will the crackers produce a Bernie? Not a cheap facsimile like that intolerable letch from Arkansas, but a true agrarian radical, a Tom Watson before his dark turn? Perhaps it's now too late, but if recent history has taught anything it is that "the agrarian question," or "the southern question," or however we should conjugate the "alliance between the working class and the peasantry" to fit the present moment, is of pressing actuality.

28

Practice. For the great theorists of the Third International (above all Gramsci), the party—and here I mean the Communist Party in its various national iterations—had an intellectual significance that is difficult to grasp from the perspective of the current period. Problems that appear in the social sciences today as purely methodological, such as that of interpretation (the relationship between scientific and lay categories) or that of causality, were treated by men like Gramsci as political problems. For example, in Gramsci interpretation appears as the problem of how to translate Marxism into a popular language of class, as well as how to translate the popular language back into Marxism. This is a political issue: it is the issue of how to develop class consciousness as the consciousness of class. Similarly, Gramsci treated the issue of causality as a matter of revolutionary strategy. Hypotheses were tested not through regression analysis, but through the history of the successes and failures of the party's strategy. (This is why the history of parties had such an important place for Gramsci.) The great intellectual advantage of this approach was that methodological conundrums, when translated into political problems, emerged in a soluble form, even if they were not solved. There is an important lesson to be extracted from this historical experience. It is that all, or most, methodological problems in the social sciences are in reality political problems posed in a mystified and therefore insoluble form. (This can only be considered a promissory note here.) The conclusion, paradoxical as it might sound, is that the scientific pretensions of sociology and its allied disciplines can be realized only in the context of a militant political agency (the party) that can actually test the hypotheses that such disciplines put forward. We could put it this way: between observation and experiment there lies the general method appropriate to the social sciences—politics.

29

-isms. We now have something as close to a doctrinal statement of Trumpism as we are likely to get: *The 1776 Report*, published in the waning days of the administration. The owl of Minerva and so on. The report was released to howls of indignation from academia and the liberal press. Its two most egregious sins were its inclusion of progressivism (alongside fascism and communism) among the great enemies of American constitutional democracy,

and its absurd treatment of slavery as destined to disappear through the imminent force of the divinely sanctioned claim to human equality embodied in the Declaration of Independence.

These objections are mostly obvious and pertinent. However, it should be noted that the critique of progressivism as the United States's analogue to fascism has a radical pedigree. Gabriel Kolko made exactly this point in *Main Currents in Modern American History*. Is it possible that Kolko's work had some subterranean influence on the report through the mediation of Murray Rothbard? What is really striking though is how utterly conventional most of the document is. Students should read the Declaration of Independence, the Constitution, and the Federalist Papers— who could object? Furthermore, do any of the liberal critics of *The 1776 Report* have any fundamental objection to the idea that the twentieth century was a conflict between US constitutionalism and the twin evils of fascism and Marxist communism?

One point that does seem distinctive to the report, and which has elicited almost no reaction, is its particular interpretation of Marxism. Marx's *Manifesto* makes an appearance in the main part of the text, as do the names of Gramsci and Marcuse in an appendix on "identity politics"; such citations are presumably a rarity in official White House publications. In what does Marx and his followers' baleful influence consist? Not in their critique of capitalism (the term does not appear), but in their supposed espousal of "group rights" that forms the intellectual foundation of "identity politics." Per the report, Marx's notion of class struggle was translated, under the combined influence of Gramsci and Marcuse, into the notion of racial struggle, both opposed to the notion of individual rights espoused by the founding fathers. This points to an important feature of the current political struggle: the clash between the Trumpists and their "woke" opponents is, for the most part, not being fought on the ground of political economy. Capitalism remains a neutral background on which conflicts over justice, freedom, and equality are fought; this perhaps explains why *The 1776 Report* makes no attempt to counter the arguments of bourgeois society's greatest critic.

30

Popper. The reflections in note 28 need concretization, an effort I begin here. Consider the problem of the state. Schematically there are three ways of understanding the modern state: either as a state of the capitalist class (Marx), an organization of legal-rational domination (Weber), or a crystallization of society's collective conscience (Durkheim). How could one begin to decide which of the three "understandings" is correct? This is a very difficult problem since much evidence supports all of these positions. Perhaps it is merely a scholastic waste of time to debate the empirical validity of such general claims. Upon further consideration, however, the Marxist theory differs in a very crucial way from its Weberian and Durkheimian counterparts. In particular it offers a different interpretation of legality. For Weber and Durkheim, the law (interpreted either as a form of command and obedience, or as condensation of a more diffused set of common norms) constitutes the modernity of the modern state. But the Marxist theory has a more differentiated view. Law reigns in "normal times," but law is suspended when the class struggle reaches that critical point during which the existing relations of property become a stake in the struggle between exploited and exploiter. During such periods a regime of exception emerges that has either a reactionary or revolutionary character. This debate can be formulated in a set of statements that potentially allow for severe empirical tests. What are these statements?

ଓ

The Marxist Theory:

(1) The state is the state of the capitalist class.
(2) If a serious political organization threatens to assume power and socialize the means of production, then the legal regime under which the state normally operates will be suspended.
(3) There are no instances of a legal transition to socialism.

The Weberian or Durkheimian Theory:

(1) The state is either a legal-rational organization or a crystallization of the common conscience.
(2) If a serious political organization threatens to assume power and socialize the means of production, then the legal regime under which the state normally operates will continue to operate.
(3) There is at least one instance of a legal transition to socialism.

What these statements show is the methodological centrality of attempts to socialize the means of production within capitalism for understanding the character of the modern state (that is, whether it is capitalist, or not). It turns out, in short, that this is not a definitional debate at all but an empirically tractable one. But how can it be studied empirically? What needs to be considered are all serious attempts to establish collective ownership through legal means within the framework of a reasonably consolidated capitalism. If any such attempt were to succeed—none have, of course—the Marxist theory of the state would be falsified through the logic of the *modus tollens* (if p implies q and q is false, then p is also false). But in fact, the Marxist theory of the state enjoys a high degree of corroboration, because it has withstood repeated attempts to falsify it in historical reality. On the other hand, there is no decisive evidence verifying either the Durkheimian or the Weberian theories (although there is also no evidence, from this way of posing the issue, of falsifying them either). Indeed, these theories, precisely because of their laxity, do not possess the degree of empirical content (that is to say, the number of factual situations which, if found, would falsify them) that the Marxist theory possesses.

How does this link to the issue of politics as the method of the social sciences? The history of left-wing social democracy is the strategic research material for understanding the "character" of the modern state. That is because left-wing social democracy is the actual attempt to violate, and in that way to test,* the Marxian universal statement, particularly in its "there is no ..." form ("there is no legal transition to socialism"). The trial of political strength is therefore the "method" by which the actual structure of the modern state—the state of the capitalist class—stands revealed. There are other examples of this sort of thing, but they all follow this general logic: structural features stand revealed only in relationship to collective political projects that aim to transform them in a particular way. There are many paradoxes that follow from this view. But these need other notes to fully explore.

---

* The Italian word *provare* gets to the meaning of what I'm after here. It means both to "prove" and "try."

31

Reality. "In this house we believe science is real." The sign is ubiquitous in the affluent progressive neighborhoods around the Bay Area and presumably around the country. Is the irony unconscious? Are the sign's displayers unaware of the jarring juxtaposition of belief and science, the latter activity presumably defined by its independence from belief? Or is the position more sophisticated? Perhaps what the sign says is that we "in this house" are aware that belief in the reality of science is one belief among others, but we choose to believe in it; in any case a whole set of symbolic oppositions that much of twentieth-century theorizing seemed bent on blurring have reemerged with considerable political force: fact/opinion, religion/science, subjective/objective. But what is the line of demarcation between these terms? The question is rarely posed, especially in discussions of the media that bemoan the decline of fact-based journalism and the expansion of opinion. But factual statements are claims about states of affairs, and as such are fallible. Conversely, opinions are, by their very form, based on an assessment of what is the case, and therefore cannot be merely private or subjective.

But one of the characteristics of American culture, particularly in the current period, is that "facts" and "opinions" are conceived as existing in unmediated opposition. Each to its own sphere. This leads on the one hand to a narcissistic fetishization of one's own opinions, and on the other to a dumb admiration for quantities of various sorts. The forms of the latter are various and familiar: batting averages, shooting percentages, fuel tank capacities, stock and citation indices. The missing link between the two is critical rationality, especially as applied to politics. For that would entail the very non-American idea that one's political views could just turn out to be mistaken—a supposition that reads like a category mistake in the land of the free.

32

Everyday people. AOC's position on the recent GameStop "squeeze," engineered by a group of small investors organized on a subreddit, exemplifies some major weaknesses of US-style democratic socialism. The congresswoman criticized Robinhood, the online trading platform that the Redditors were using, for limiting trading after the emergence of an obvious speculative bubble overvaluing the dying brick-and-mortar store GameStop. AOC called, in a tweet, for a probe into Robinhood, and quickly found unwelcome support from Ted Cruz and Newt Gingrich. (Interestingly, Elizabeth Warren had a much more measured response, citing the events as evidence of systemic problems and calling for greater regulation of the stock market.) What explains AOC's odd reaction to these events? In her own words, "People were really feeling like everyday people were finally able to collectively organize and get back at the folks who have historically had all the marbles on Wall Street."

The problems here are at once conceptual and political. "Everyday people"—do you mean the multimillionaire investor who was one of the originators of the scheme? "Collectively organize"—do you mean a scheme to push a stock value artificially high, a process that will lead to the inevitable ruin of many small-scale investors? And what about "folks who have historically had all the marbles"? As if the problem were the distribution of the "marbles" and not the absurd system of betting through which a considerable portion of the country's, and indeed the world's, social surplus is allocated. The AOC position is not idiosyncratic; rather, it expresses a deeper problem: the basically legalistic framework within which the new US social democratic left as a whole moves. This left conceives the fundamental flaw of US society to be one of unfairness and injustice: monopoly power, concentrated wealth, a "rigged" political system.

All these ideas are concentrated in the term "social justice." The problem with this essentially forensic diagnosis is that all of its demands are perfectly compatible with private ownership of society's main productive assets, as well as, more importantly, the private determination of society's investment decisions. To avoid bizarre entanglements and false alliances, the US left should talk much less about making society "fairer" (a muddled and basically petit bourgeois notion) and much more about making society more rational or human. For after all, isn't the goal of every serious socialist the subordination of the blind processes of second nature—and perhaps in our day we should add the brutal vengeance of first nature—to the will of humanity? How can the grandeur of this project be fitted into the narrow framework of fairness? It is like putting a blue whale into a fishbowl.

33

Justice. Certain arguments in Marx and Hayek bear an uncanny resemblance, in spite of their diametrically opposed politics. Both were fascinated with the blind character of social cooperation under capitalism: a society of all-round interdependence mediated by private decisions. Whereas this contradiction inspired Hayek to compose quasi-Burkean hosannas to ignorance, Marx identified it as the fundamental weakness of capitalism. Both also rejected the application of the category of justice to the social process: for Hayek because the "extended order" was a natural development, and so expecting justice from it would be akin to expecting justice from a tree or a mountain, for

Marx because justice applies to the distribution of currently
available resources, but offers no guide to the division of
the social product between current consumption and investment; there is no "socially just" structure of accumulation,
or rather there may be many, some of which are more desirable than others for reasons that have nothing to do with
justice. Noting these common points brings out with great
sharpness the real differences. All of Hayek's arguments are
based ultimately on the idea of the social as a manifestation
of the sublime, leaving the analyst in a state of dumb cre-
dulity. Marx's arguments derive from precisely the opposite
impulse: that society is a creation of the human species, and
potentially controllable by its rationality. Justice itself, being
a human creation, cannot be allowed to become a fetish: as
if the meaning of human history could be decided through
a judicial procedure, as if there were a metacourt standing outside of history. There is no "just" society in general,
and every society that has law is presumably in some sense
a "just" society. The point is not justice, but rationality—
which is to say, freedom.

34

Online teaching. It is strangely personal. The soft chime, the
colored tile sometimes replaced by a face, at other times not.
Pieces of domestic life intrude (cats, puppies, dirty dishes,
unfolded laundry). These are normally carefully excluded
from the seminar room or lecture hall. A softening of the
pedagogical relationship inevitably ensues on both sides.
Teachers and students are now bound together in the
common recognition of their absurd condition. "Was I a
little unclear?" A chat will rectify the situation, creating a
new and more informal bond with my students. "Were they
a little hesitant and inarticulate?" But it may just be a bad

connection, or an inability to fully extricate themselves from the intimate sphere into which I feel I am intruding in any case. The video chat seems to demand reciprocal generosity—in itself, perhaps, not a bad thing. But there may be another side to all this "sphere mixing," to use the colloquial expression in a slightly different way. Like a breaching experiment, or a negative case, it throws a sharp retrospective light on the preconditions and purpose of the physical organization of teaching. Think of the massive labor behind the punctual co-presence of a class: commutes, schedule organization, building maintenance, provision of services. A tiny self-reproducing packet of protein has ground all this to a halt. But what is the point? What is a university as a physical space of teaching for? (Crises force one to face the really central questions.) It is a giant structure designed temporarily to suspend social determinations—those different material conditions of existence that divide any student body, particularly at a public university—through the creation of innumerable public spheres. Of course, it fails in countless ways; but this is the purpose of co-presence. The most basic threat that video-mediated instruction poses is not that it makes communication with students more difficult or distant, but that it dissolves the boundary between the quotidian world and the world of thought. The seminar room or lecture hall is the material structure that maintains this boundary, and as such is an indispensable precondition for the rational-critical process to unfold. The threat, in short, that the current technologically mediated model poses to teaching is not that it drives students and instructors too far apart, but that it brings them paradoxically too close together, and, as it were, in the wrong way.

35

Pseudo-antitheory. The self-hating sociologist is as familiar a figure of the current intellectual landscape as her close cousin, the self-hating philosopher. The target of this type is inevitably "theory," disparaged as a body of antiquated and irrelevant texts that at one time may have been a useful magazine of "hypotheses," but which now clutters intellectual space like a collection of unloved family heirlooms that no one has the courage to take to the dump. But what is to replace them? Here the antitheorist inevitably suggests the following three claims. First, everyday explanations and concepts have just as much, if not more, analytic power as the specialized language and categories of the classics. Second, significant social relationships are immediately apparent, especially now that we are awash in such a massive sea of data that even the tools of statistical inference (especially sampling) are no longer relevant. Third, and finally, scientific progress is most clearly indicated when scientists forget the history of their own fields of inquiry. The paradox of the antitheorist's position is that each of these claims is eminently theoretical. The first says that society is transparent to its members; the second, that causal connections are directly intuitable; and the third, that the history of science is linear and progressive. What wild and unsupported metaphysical claims are these? They reveal that the antitheorist is always in fact a pseudo-antitheorist, whose metaphysical body must be extracted from the misleading positivist shell in which she shrouds herself. Only then can the quivering fragility of the metaphysics be examined in the cold light of reason and evidence.

36

Bargains. On all sides we hear of "work-life balance." Whatever work is, it is the opposite of life: death? So, these eight or ten hours of death must be balanced with a corresponding period of life. It seems like a better bargain might be struck. Has anyone thought of getting rid of work qua work?

37

Objective spirit. Where is Emanuela? She is in her chair, of course, or in the garden, or taking a walk. But she is also in all the created things that surround us, that envelop us, that care for us. The hats and scarves and blankets and mended socks and quilted things and delightful little creatures and figures. And they are all saying one thing: "Vi amo."

38

The aesthetics of politics. We Americans—those on the left as much as those on the right—are forever fighting political battles under some other name: morality, truth, religious conviction, justice. In politics we are naive children attracted by, and demanding of, qualities of our political leaders that are irrelevant or positively harmful to the pursuit of politics as a calling. A conversation with a friend of mine from Bologna, a man of the left, brought it home to me. Giorgia Meloni, he said, is a politician of the "serious" right. He appreciated her coherence in rejecting the blandishments of the new premier, Mario Draghi. It is a judgment based on the ability to disengage politics from other activities and to evaluate it in a quasi-aesthetic mode. The American left would do well to adopt a similar stance: to spend less energy on outrage and more on the study and appreciation of the laws of power and its exercise. Isn't that what Machiavelli was trying to teach us? We had better learn to listen.

39

Wilhelmine antiquity. What to do with all the Webers? There is one for every political-intellectual taste. Apostle of modernization for the liberal center; unmasker of the myth of mass democracy for the right; critic of instrumental reason and essential supplement to Marx's analysis of commodity fetishism for the left. For the academics there is Weber the methodologist, the "institutionalist" thinker *avant la lettre*, the "cultural" sociologist focused on values and meanings. There is even Weber the teacher and adviser explaining the relationship between "facts" and "values" and analyzing the travails of intellectual life. But none of these Webers is actually the one needed for the current moment. That Weber, surprising as it may sound, is the great historical analyst of classical antiquity; this is because of the reemergence of political capitalism, profit-oriented activity dependent on the possession of political power, in the late twentieth and early twenty-first century. The whole realm of finance—which now includes large chunks of what are supposedly manufacturing firms—as well as industries dependent on "intellectual property" (that is to say, on politically enforced monopolies), as well as extractive industries based on the seizure of public lands, depends on political power to ensure its economic viability. This creates a new form of politics. The state is an object of struggle among competing political-capitalist cliques. In antiquity two models emerged: the universal monarchy, which to some extent disciplined these groups; and the unstable republic, which allowed them to run rampant. Are there not analogues in the current period?

Putin's Russia could be thought of as the Roman universal monarchy, and the United States the unstable republican form.

40

Ideas and weapons. When we learn that Marx had some perhaps questionable personal habits, that for example he accepted payments from his wealthy friend and had his housekeeper as his mistress, as well a having occasionally expressed unsavory views of Jews and people of color, have we learned anything more about his ideas than we would have about the quality of a sword on the basis of studying its blacksmith's biography?

41

Myth and science. It is difficult to understand Sorel's importance, despite the efforts of generations of intellectual historians to explain it. How could his work, so much of which is so unhinged and disorganized—enumerated lists that lead to nowhere, rantings against minor and forgotten figures, infuriating political ambiguity—have been so important for giants such as Gramsci, Lukács, Schmitt, Croce, and Gentile? It may be worth the effort to sketch a provisional answer (which will inevitably appear crude, but may have heuristic value).

Orthodox Marxism opposed ideology to science. Sorel, above all in *Reflections on Violence*, opposed these contrasts with another set: myth to detachment. He then used this reorganized scheme to reinterpret Marx's *Manifesto* as a "practical-myth," thereby protecting its core idea—that capitalist society was splitting apart into two hostile class camps—from Bernstein's well-founded argument that, in fact, it was not. If, per Sorel, the *Manifesto* was a myth, then its "truth" (or practical utility) consisted in its rhetorical power, its ability to make the working class believe in the story it told.

Sorel is important not because of this, in many ways absurd, answer to Bernstein. His importance derives, instead, from the fact that he identified, or stumbled upon, what became one of the central problems of Western Marxism: the relationship of Marxist theory to working-class consciousness. But Sorel's tools for solving this problem (Bergsonian philosophy and Durkheimian sociology) were utterly inadequate. Gramsci, who was an arch-rationalist, went the furthest in sketching a solution. He suggested that the opposition between science and myth could be resolved in the political party, the Modern Prince that is supposed to replace Sorel's myth. He was convinced that in the context of the party, reason had a greater persuasive power than myth; thus, science could be practical in precisely the sense that Sorel said it could not. This firm belief in the persuasive power of rational explanation is often forgotten in culturalist interpretations of Gramsci, which tend to portray him as a neo-Sorelian, even if they don't use this language, when he had in fact only taken over a problem from Sorel and given it an entirely different solution.

42

Hintze. Otto Hintze could be understood as Weber's Engels. (There are of course differences. Weber and Hintze were politically quite distinct, the first a bourgeois "National Liberal," the second a monarchist and "socialist of the chair." They did not have the close working relationship that Marx and Engels had; but for heuristic purposes the parallel is useful.) Just as Engels concretized Marx's sprawling corpus, so Hintze focused and developed Weber's historical sociology, particularly his historical sociology of the state. This is not to diminish Hintze's originality—nor Engels's for that matter. Indeed, Hintze anticipated much of Weber's theory of bureaucracy, just as Engels anticipated Marx's *Contribution to the Critique of Political Economy*. In any case, Hintze's significance is hard to overstate; the vast majority of Anglo-American writing on state formation (Skocpol, Tilly, and more recently Downing, Ertman, and Gorski, a group often generically referred to as neo-Weberian) is little more than a footnote to his work. Every central thesis of this literature—that states are "autonomous" from classes, that war is the driving force in state formation, that medieval constitutionalism is the basis of the modern representative state, and that Calvinism stands at the origin of modern bureaucracy—is already well developed in Hintze.

One reason why this may not be more widely known in the United States is that Hintze's major work, *Die Hohenzollern und ihr Werk*, remains untranslated. What did Hintze accomplish? First, he clarified the conceptual and political stakes of the debate on the state. The claim that states form not in relation to "intrasocietal" class struggle, but to the "extrasocietal" struggle for existence among political communities, was developed as a systematic alternative to "social democratic" history—that is, Marxism. Second, he laid the foundations for an actual historical sociology of European state formation, a task that Weber never completed.

But Hintze's work differed in important respects from Weber's. For Weber was not a proponent of the primacy of Aussenpolitik nor was he a theorist of "state autonomy." On the contrary, like Marx, Weber saw a deep internal relationship between capitalism and the modern state. Indeed, for Weber the link is actually more intimate than for Marx, because he held that a fully developed capitalist economy was the precondition for the separation of the officeholder from the office that forms the specific characteristic of the modern state at the molecular-political level. (Neither Marx nor Engels of course developed more than a rudimentary account of bureaucracy.) It is the ability of the bureaucratic chief to fire the subordinate official that is the ultimate guarantee of legal-rational domination. Of course, this raises exactly the same problem that Marx faced: the obvious noncoincidence between the development of the modern state and the development of modern capitalism (see Britain). Perhaps the way to pose the problem is as the intersection of two processes of expropriation: the expropriation of the official of the means of administration, and the expropriation of the direct producers of the means of production. But how these processes are linked in theory and historical reality remains without a convincing answer.

43

Sticking together. How to link the problem of solidarity to class analysis? Reading Brenner makes the importance of this question clear. Evidently the problem of the "transition from feudalism to capitalism" for Brenner concerns the connections among class struggles, class formation, and class structure. But it becomes clear as one reads that the real key to the different outcomes in different parts of Europe is solidarity: highly solidary lordly communities in post-Norman England, together with somewhat individualistic peasants (capitalism); highly solidary peasants in fifteenth-century France, together with a fractious nobility (absolutism); weakly solidary peasants in East Elbian Germany, together with highly solidary lords (second serfdom). Indeed, the terms "community" and "solidarity" recur repeatedly throughout the work.

What is Brenner's explanation of these different levels of

solidarity within different social classes? He has an answer:
class struggle. But we might turn Brenner's style of critique
of the demographic and commercial models against his
own work at precisely this point: why would similar class
struggles in different parts of Europe lead to such different outcomes in terms of the relative levels of solidarity
among peasants and lords? What Brenner does not have,
but clearly requires, is a theory of solidarity within different
social classes.

This specific issue, not resolvable in the space of a note,
raises the general question of what a class is, and should be
linked to Gramsci's note on intellectuals. For what Gramsci
saw, especially when he spoke of classes as having "spe-
cializations," is that classes are neither abstract locations
nor groups: they are, instead, structures of social solidarity.
Gramsci's note on intellectuals sketches an "organic" form
of intraclass solidarity that recalls, though perhaps falsely,
Durkheim's organic solidarity based on the division of labor.
(There is no evidence that I am aware of that Gramsci ever
read Durkheim.) Bourdieu also speaks toward the end of his
book entitled *The State Nobility* of the "organic solidarity"
of the dominant class. Poulantzas also suggests the idea
that the differentiation of the various fractions of the capitalist class promoted their cohesion through cooperation.
(It is remarkable how profoundly Durkheimian the whole
structuralist tradition is from Althusser through Poulantzas
to Bourdieu.)

Perhaps the following broad hypothesis would be worth
investigating: in precapitalist societies classes take the form
of "communities" of relatively similar types of persons. Durkheim would have termed such communities mechanically
solidary. Under capitalism, however, classes take the form
of a social structure of solidarity based on difference and
the division of labor. Is there any better example of organic
solidarity than the capitalist class, with all its divisions and
intermeshing segments? There are also fractions or segments

of classes among the direct producers: workers in factories, on the land, in commerce, and in services. Durkheim then could be rescued from all his apologetic followers if it were pointed out that he offers not a theory of social solidarity, but a theory of class solidarity in a social order divided by relations of exploitation.

44

Betwixt and between. O that happy little amphibian, the "empirical democratic theorist." When the conceptual sun becomes too hot, he can dive into the cool waters of the empirical pool. When the pool gets too cloudy and cool, he clambers out to dry again in the restorative rays of normative debate. But he must be ever darting to and fro so as not to be caught by the impossible question, "And, why, pray tell, is it just these arrangements that you identify with the people's will?" Otherwise, he will wither like a salamander in the desert.

45

The dogma of implicitness. "Why teach social theory?" The question is perhaps badly posed. Just as it is impossible in sociological research not to theorize, so it is impossible to teach sociology without teaching social theory. The real choice differs; it is between the teaching of theory as a specific topic and the teaching of theory as something implicit, something that will emerge from the study of other problems. So, to reformulate, we should ask, "Why teach social theory explicitly as a topic?" The best way to answer this question is to turn it around to ask, "What theory of society must one hold to have the view that social theory should not be taught explicitly as a topic?" Evidently it is a theory stating that society is transparent to its members. The study of society requires, from this point of view, neither a specialized language, nor a specialized approach to formulating problems. Instead, the language and the problems can be taken directly from everyday experience. This may be right, or it may be wrong—or, my view, it may be right at some periods and for some groups, and wrong for other periods and other groups. But in order to know whether the theory that supports the nonteaching of theory is right or wrong, it would have to be developed *as a theory*, and it would have to be explicitly compared with alternative theories in terms of its internal coherence and empirical implications. The point, then, is this: even the person most committed to the implicit teaching of theory must have some answer to the question about why this teaching should be implicit, and that answer in turn will be theoretical in the sense that it will be based on a social theory. To sum up, unless we are in the business of passing off our views as religious dogmas, we had better explicitly teach social theory as a topic, especially if we think we should not be.

46

Office. "From the Office of Donald J. Trump," with a presidential seal underneath: the new letterhead of the ex-occupant of the White House. Doubtless this odd title is the result of a compromise between those not willing to openly declare a situation of dual power and others leery of antagonizing their chief by referring to him as an ex-president. But it unintentionally reveals the basic novelty of Trump: his radical denial of any distinction between office and occupant. "Office" in the sense of "From the Office of Donald J. Trump" refers not to an "office"—since presumably there is no such thing as a position named "Donald J. Trump" occupiable by different persons, as

with the names, in Mauss's description, that can endure
after their holders have passed—but rather to the room in
which the letter was composed. It is this profoundly anti-
bureaucratic personalization of domination that stands as
the most distinctive political feature of Trump.

47

Therapeutics. The previous note on social theory (note
45) will seem perhaps overly abstract. Can a more
straightforward justification be provided? Social theory's
most basic purpose is to denaturalize the social world. That
world now appears to be what it in fact is: an instance of
a possible social world among two or more possible such
worlds (capitalism rather than feudalism; legal-rational
rather than traditional authority; organic rather than
mechanical solidarity; urban civilization rather than desert
civilization). The point is to use the contrasts between total
social types to force the listener into a mode of questioning:
"Why do I work for a wage, when others clearly do not?"
"Why is there not constant civil war?" "Why are there so
many mediocrities in power with all the incessant chatter
about the value of education?" "Why are so many talents
wasted?" "Why are mass murderers and their apologists
rewarded with posts in academia, when petty hustlers are
locked away for years?" It is possible that such queries might
arise in the normal course of affairs, stumbled over like
rocks that trip the absent-minded walker. But the peculiar
intellectual product called social theory imposes them with
tremendous force.

How does it work its magic? By drawing the reader into
the perspective of an outsider to the given social arrange-
ment. We ought to consider in this regard the peculiar
biographical/historical conditions that have produced the
great social theories. Durkheim, Du Bois, and Marx were

all ethnic minorities, Marx and Khaldun were immigrants, Weber was isolated and mentally ill. Furthermore, and this is often not sufficiently registered, none of the foremost social theorists lived in fully consolidated capitalist societies. Khaldun's Mediterranean presented massive contrasts between the rich trading region of the East and the less commercialized West. The United States in the nineteenth century closely resembled the German Reich in its weird combination of industrial capitalism and semifeudal cash crop agriculture. France, despite its great-power pretensions, was saddled with a backward agrarian sector until well after the Second World War (a paradoxical legacy of the Great Revolution).

It is the combination, in short, of this outsider perspective with the possibility of making these direct and total contrasts that allowed for the emergence of a social science that was at once denaturalizing and totalizing (the two things are inextricably linked). Social theory, especially in its "classical" form, can be thought of as offering a perspective that is otherwise extremely difficult to attain in the hyperdeveloped capitalisms of the post-1945 world, which is spontaneously antitheoretical. That is why we teach social theory; it is one powerful therapy for the mental disorder of reification.

48

Ideas. One must insist, particularly from the perspective of materialism, on the reality of ideas. It is necessary to emphasize this in the current period, dominated as it is by a crude sociology of knowledge, already discussed in note 15, that reduces thought to the expression of biography (or to put the point in a way sociologists might understand, "positionality"). A more sophisticated version of this move, common among Bourdieusians, is to interpret all claims as "stance-taking" in a field. Usually a flat relativism praising different "perspectives" ensues (which Bourdieu of course tried to escape, but only by embracing a dubious ideology of professionalization). This is a vague echo of John Stuart Mill, but without the hard-hitting critical edge of his work.

The real connections among biography, history, and thought are far more complex than either of these models can grasp. A few basic points should be firmly kept in mind. First, it is possible to understand an idea, and indeed to grasp and use it as a tool of thought and struggle, while knowing little to nothing about its producer's biography. This is not to say that such knowledge might not be helpful, but it is at least relatively superfluous. Second, it ought to be absolutely clear that the "position" of the idea's author has no bearing at all on the question of whether the idea is true or false, coherent or incoherent, useful or useless. Confusion on this point shows a lack of understanding about the realm of reality that one is dealing with in "the world of ideas."

Having said this, one very important question— addressed by a variety of thinkers from widely different political and intellectual standpoints, and with a sophistica- tion and seriousness that utterly eludes the contemporary sociology of knowledge—concerns the explanation for the kinds of social conditions that produce ideas that are true, coherent, and useful, or on the contrary false, incoherent, or useless. (Durkheim and Lukács might still stand as two towering examples of at least an attempt to address the issue.) The relativism that pervades the sociology of knowl- edge in its current form, and which has also become part of the mental formation of a wide swathe of academia, has dissolved the entire basis of this central question. In its place have emerged more or less sophisticated citation counts, which present themselves as studies in the "social con- struction of knowledge," without ever saying clearly what knowledge is. (There is a very strange convergence between the bureaucratic-quanto tendency and various more or less pomo, or more precisely neo-Kantian, epistemological positions.) This general situation leads to a corrosive skepticism about both the production of knowledge and its teaching. Now it's all of course about production and transmission of "cultural capital": an anticoncept that is choking the humanities and the social sciences like the kudzu that spread with the railroads all over the US South. American higher education is becoming a vast apparatus devoted to avoiding the serious discussion of ideas.

49

Elitism. Devotion to the demos and hatred of "elites" is perhaps the only commitment shared across the otherwise profoundly polarized political and cultural landscape. From commercial textbook sales reps peddling "gamified" courses suited to the short attention spans of today's students, to aspiring PhDs outraged at the "elitist" practices of academia, to the ubiquitous fetishists of false clarity who are forever on the lookout for too many subordinate clauses and ideas not diagrammable with two circles and one arrow, to right-wing bloviators attacking "coastal elites": it seems, in fact, that no one is standing up for the elites these days. (On the right, the *New Criterion*, and on the left, *n+1*, are like fragile sandcastles in the surf in this regard.) And yet, in the midst of so much fervent chest-thumping on behalf of the little guy or gal, never in its history has wealth and income been so unequally distributed in American society. What is going on? It is worth noting that the primary targets of all this anti-elitism are cultural (above all people who write books and articles). Which raises a question: Is there not a subterranean collusion between the disciplining populism that pervades both left and right, and the requirements of accumulation? As if difficult ideas themselves were obstacles to the smooth circulation of commodities, like the variously sized packages that used to waste space on freighters before the invention of the shipping container.

50

Equality. Does the embrace of socialism require a commitment to equality? The question seems nonsensical, especially in the United States, where a vague and shifting line separates "radical democratic egalitarianism" and democratic socialism. But it must be said that the classics were far from full throated in their endorsement of equality. Fourier, of course, with his insistence on differences of wealth within the "Progressive Household," but also Marx, who seems to have thought, especially in the *Critique of the Gotha Programme*, that equality is an inherently contradictory idea. To treat unequals equally will reinforce inequality, whereas to treat unequals unequally is clearly inequitable. Furthermore, the famous phrase "From each according to his ability, to each according to his needs" hardly seems like an endorsement of equality. What, after all, if people's needs are different? This does not mean that socialism could ever be inegalitarian; that would be an idiotic and paradoxical claim. It seems, rather, that socialism, or the humanized society, points to a form that is somehow beyond equality and inequality. This is so because it would be a society allowing for an absolute flourishing of individuality, where people are neither equal to one another, nor unequal to one another; they are instead irreducibly unique (which is why life is tragic). In the humanized society we could say that the concepts of equality and inequality will be relegated "to the museum of antiquities, next to the spinning wheel and the bronze ax."

51

Books. They are out of sorts today. Glaring down at me in serried, multicolored ranks. Each one full of promise, with its own particular take and structure; its highly personal merits and foibles. Each the product of a titanic struggle; and each having caused God knows how many sleepless nights and domestic disputes. This morning they are murmuring, complaining of the dust and general neglect. They probably suffer from allergies. The product of so much human effort and creativity, they demand one thing: to be given their due and read.

52

Class and nation. Occasionally one hears "class identity" as a term to indicate an equivalence between it and racial and gender identities. This is a serious confusion. For the concept of identity refers to a tangible, or phenomenal, reality. Races, ethnicities, and genders generate experiential "group feelings." This does not mean they are subjective. The observation that a given identity is "socially constructed" does not mean one is free to choose one's identity. A whole set of political, ideological, and bureaucratic structures pin me as a white male, no matter what I think about the matter. But identities of these sorts exist in a phenomenal/experiential realm.

Class differs. Of course, at certain moments, in certain societies, class can be experienced or intuited; but this is precisely an indicator of relative backwardness. Think of what Anderson says about the bourgeoisie being identifiable by the wearing of hats: an outward sign which has now disappeared. Now we have Zuckerberg's slovenly hoodies and bad haircut. Gramsci grasped the central point (again, it is a major mystery to me how he managed to see so far ahead). Classes under advanced capitalism are typically not culturally marked: they do not have identities. This is obviously one of the most significant factors leading to the reproduction of capitalism. There are national cultures, but to an increasing degree there is no class culture. (Obviously Gellner saw this point as well. In many respects his ideas converge with Gramsci.)

To take the full significance of this point requires a profound break with the whole line of class analysis that grew out of Thompson and, in a different way, Bourdieu. Despite all their obvious differences, *Distinction* and *The Making of the English Working Class* resemble each other in one important way: they demonstrate exactly the opposite of what their authors intended. Both show the immense power of the national/bourgeois culture and the surprising weakness of any real cultural boundaries between classes. To put it bluntly, Bourdieu showed that French workers were going to museums, Thompson that English workers were stuffed to the gills with the ideas of bourgeois radicals like Thomas Paine and William Cobbett and classical political economists, especially David Ricardo. But generations of scholars have followed the explicit intent of these works, producing a vast sea of studies of culture and class. What should be done instead is to read Bourdieu and Thompson against themselves as a way of recovering Gramsci's initial insight: the culture of capitalism is precisely a universal culture that destroys the reality of class at the phenomenal level. Classes then tend ever more to exist as structural positions whose effects must be inferred, rather than as directly intuitable identities. Or, to put the Gramscian point in Weber's language, classes are definitely not now *Stände*, and the role of parties is to make them such.

53

Little stories. Claims do not exist anymore; "narratives" have replaced them. What accounts for this odd transformation of language? Doubtless it is a general effect of postmodernism—according to Google Ngram Viewer, use of "narrative" began to spike in the early 1980s. But the intrusion of the word into middlebrow culture, the space of NPR or the *NYT* in the United States, seems more recent. Is it the delayed effect of so many years of teaching Lyotard, his language now finally having seeped into the *forma mentis* of the average journalist? In any case its chloroforming function is quite remarkable. Narratives are either "pushed" or "pushed back on." Unlike claims, they are not investigated, shown to be either compatible or incompatible with the available evidence. It is true that we often hear of "false narratives." But the modifier sits oddly with the noun; how exactly can a story be either true or false? More commonly, the journalist assumes a stance of pseudosophisticated relativism, reporting on the various "competing narratives" (as if all the world were a market for mediocre fiction). This too is an example of the potency of theory, but in this case it is a force that enervates and blinds rather than strengthens and enlightens.

54

Sunk costs. It is hard to avoid the impression that "canonical" struggles are really a misrecognized clash of quite specific material interests. The importance of "sunk costs" in academic life should never be underestimated. Every professor has a large stock of written materials, images, graphs, reading notes, and ready-to-hand interpretations that she has accumulated over years of study and thought. Although one really must avoid the slipshod analogies encouraged by the term "cultural capital," these artifacts have a certain resemblance to "fixed capital" in the Marxian lexicon. They provide a basic framework through which new information can be easily digested or "valorized." In a material sense, a challenge to the "canon" poses the threat of the rapid devaluation of fixed assets. The rational response of these asset holders is "to stand and fight," to preserve the value of their assets even if their intellectual equipment is somewhat dated. They can at least make good use of it to valorize their "circulating capital." The challengers in a material sense have quite opposite interests. They would like to leapfrog the incumbents and set up shop on the basis of an entirely new set of fixed endowments. This is the material meaning of the various projects of syllabus revision underway across the sprawling complex of US higher education, although ideologically this campaign is carried out under the sign of "decolonizing the syllabus" or similar slogans.

A couple of observations about this struggle are in order. First, it is important to point out the limits of the analogy. For in academic life there is no field of natural selection operating to weed out less efficient producers (as much as the managers of the neoliberal university would like this to be the case). Nor is there any analogue to exploitation. Second, the highly paradoxical character of the conflict should be emphasized. The most conservative actors in any struggle over the canon are likely to be in the least prestigious positions with the fewest opportunities to retool. To make matters worse, these are also the actors most likely to be the most vulnerable to negative student evaluations and the bureaucratic apparatus. Thus, we can fully expect that the costs of "decolonizing the syllabus" will be borne by those least able to bear them. Conversely those likely to win the most from the struggle will be those actors most well placed, with the lowest teaching loads and the most time to retool. The openness of this stratum to student demands for transformation is largely an index of its academic privilege. The outcome, in any case, will hardly be an overthrow of the canon, but a heightening of "barriers of entry" for all players. A final note to the reader: the message of this note is contained both in what it says and in how it says it.

55

Potenza. My son Eamon's cello sings: Tchaikovsky, Brahms, Bach, and Haydn. His sound has grown with him like his muscles and his hair: strong and sinewy, precise and confident. The cello is no longer a challenge and a chore; it is now another voice with which to speak. It speaks of hope and fear, of anger and love, of joy and frustration: all with an intensity proper to youth, in comparison with which the emotions of middle age seem like so many exhausted shades. It is potency, but also potentiality: an exquisite balance between the fine thing that is and the possibility of what is to come. Like a beautifully clear dawn that promises a long and joy-filled summer day.

56

Bourgeois revolution? One of the most enduring myths of US history writing and political analysis is that the Civil War, by laying the groundwork for the Thirteenth, Fourteenth, and Fifteenth Amendments (abolition of slavery, guarantee of equal protection, and guarantee of the right to vote), "saved" or "delivered on the promise of" American democracy. A few facts should be recalled in this regard, and the problem placed in an appropriate comparative setting. In the first place, the "superstructural" changes that issued from the cataclysm were minuscule; the most important ones, the amendments mentioned above, were largely dead letters after 1876 in the region in which they were meant to apply. The constitutional republic established in 1789 was there before and after the massive bloodletting of the war itself: a remarkable fact, especially if compared with the really substantial changes ushered in by supposedly conservative modernizing processes such as German and Italian unification and the Meiji Restoration.

Secondly, to describe the Civil War as a revolution in any sense is to stretch the term beyond use. The argument was most powerfully developed by Du Bois in *Black Reconstruction*, a book that among other things aimed to restore the historical agency of the formerly enslaved. But however important the flight of the ex-slaves toward the Union lines was in an economic sense, it cannot be described as a moment of collective political agency such as the *journées* of the French Revolution, the Haitian uprising, or the Paris Commune. The social axis of the American Civil War was a split among the main factions of the US dominant class: the populace, white and Black, mostly played the part of cannon fodder.

What of the social outcome? Did the Civil War "modernize" the United States? The abolition of slavery had two main consequences. First, in place of large units of cultivation worked by gang labor, a system of small-scale cultivation worked by individual families emerged. Second, the landowners lost a huge part of their capital base (the enslaved) and as a result were largely excluded from financial markets. (Credit is absolutely fundamental to agriculture.) What emerged out of the struggle among freedmen, planters, and merchants was the system of sharecropping. This was hardly capitalist agriculture; indeed, in terms of what one could call the "relations in production" (Burawoy), it was a step back from the more complex division of labor that characterized slavery. As Jaynes's fundamental book *Branches without Roots* implies, a more "progressive solution" to the agrarian problem would have been to maintain the large units of cultivation under collective ownership. Sharecropping had many negative consequences, especially for women who were subjected to a system of patriarchal surveillance. The whole system, in any case, kept the South in a state of semidependency for decades. The real economic achievement of the war was the extension of the East/West axis on which American capitalist development depended. (The final elimination of the indigenous population was another major outcome of the Civil War.)

The spread of sharecropping among both whites and Blacks in the South had, in any case, important political consequences. Combined with the reinvigorated racial "caste spirit" (Du Bois), it acted as a massive barrier to the establishment of any effective alliance among agrarian and urban workers, as evidenced by the repeated failures of popular mobilization from the Populist movement to the thirties. As the obverse of the same factors that weakened intraclass solidarity, the now impoverished southern plantocracy could never wield the agrarian population as a *masse de manoeuvre* to create a rightist mass politics. There was no analogue to the Bund der Landwirte. Note well: this is hardly because the Civil War had solved the "peasant problem"; in fact if anything it had created a quasi-peasantry where none existed before. It was instead the result of the racial caste system itself. Thus, what allowed for the constitutional republic's smooth transition to the twentieth century was not its pluralistic openness, but the very opposite: its imperviousness to any substantial pressure from the working masses, white or Black. This too was an achievement of the Civil War.

57

Collection. The thoughts come to me like butterflies, or bees, or hummingbirds. They stay for just a moment before flitting away, crowded out by obligations and worries of various sorts. I have taken to pinning them down. What will the product of all this be? Perhaps simply a collection like those wooden boxes of insects, birds, teeth, or fossils that one used to see at natural history museums. Or better put, the notes are more like what these collections must have looked like before their organization according to size and shape, genus and species. For now, they exist in absolute diachrony: what came before, and what came after.

58

Underclass. "The fallacy of misplaced cultural specificity" is a phrase likely to appeal only to sociologists, and only to a few of them at that. Still, it describes an important phenomenon, one that links the discussion of "culture and class" in note 52 with the idea of the "culture of poverty" or "culture of the underclass" deriving from discussions of the urban poor, especially the African American urban poor. The lines of debate run something like the following. One group claims that the problems of the underclass are partially a consequence of their culture: individualism, heedlessness, lack of marital stability. The other group claims that the problems are structural, deriving from a lack of resources, not cultural deficiency. Doubtless, the second group has the stronger argument, and is at least relatively free from the moralizing essentialism that runs from Charles Booth's studies of the London poor all the way to the Moynihan Report and beyond. But there may be a more productive point to be made here.

A closer look at the evidence, for example in William Julius Wilson's later work, shows the urban poor espousing platitudes about the importance of self-reliance, express- ing desire for gewgaws (expensive cars and jewelry), and embracing a consumerist ethos. Culture of poverty? This is just the narcissistic culture of US capitalism, with its somewhat distinctive fetishization of the consumer. It is hard, therefore, to escape the impression that the entire problem of "culture" has been very wrongly posed here. The question is definitely not why and with what consequences the culture of the urban poor differs from "mainstream" culture, but rather, why it is so similar to it. (It should be obvious that this is exactly the same problem that plagues Bourdieu's *Distinction*, which suffers from asking the wrong question of its empirical material. A certain kind of national parochialism, American and French, respectively, lies behind this common error.) It is here that Gramsci's notion of hegemony is clarifying and can be put into relationship with the history of the Black Power movement.

For, speaking broadly, what was this movement? Its filiation with Maoism was certainly no accident, nor its earlier attachment to Islam. Black Power was an incipient cultural revolution: the attempt to create a national culture that could insulate African Americans from the circumambient white culture. It failed for a number of reasons, including the lack of an adequate territorial base and/or alternative language, and the extraction of the Black bourgeoisie and petite bourgeoisie (the strata who are always the "natural bearers" of nationalism) from the urban centers, as documented by Wilson, inter alia. State repression also played an obvious role. Thus, the social foundations of an *autonomous* Black nationalism either did not exist or were undermined. The "culture of the underclass" emerged precisely after the destruction of this attempt, and represents not a cultural specificity, but rather a process of cultural homogenization; hence, "the fallacy of misplaced cultural specificity."

59

Circuits. If one were asked to express how Marx saw capitalist society's account of itself, and how that account differs from the real character of capitalism, the place to start would be his schemes of circulation. The circuit of simple commodity production (illustrated by the formula C-M-C), in which a commodity is exchanged for money, which is then exchanged for a commodity of a different sort, describes not just a type of economy (petty commodity production), but more importantly a way of experiencing capitalist society. The vast majority of the population in any capitalist society is inserted into the economy through the C-M-C circuit. Thus, the most natural way to regard all other persons under capitalism is to consider them just as other petty producers and sellers of commodities. Of course, Marx's point is that the reality of capitalism differs entirely from this; it is characterized by a circuit in which money is exchanged for commodities, which are then resold for more money after being combined with means of production and labor.

We can state the relationship of capitalism's real character —or to put it a bit pretentiously, its essence—to the way in which the society is experienced by most people this way: a society that is really dominated by M-C-M' is experienced as if it were a society of petty commodity producers. Petit bourgeois ideology is then an ideology that describes a society driven by the accumulation of surplus value as if it were a society of small-scale traders; and it describes the immediate, everyday appearance of capitalism to most people who live in this type of society.

To see how relevant this analysis is, it is enough to consider the democratic socialist left's critique of capitalism, made mostly by persons who would bristle at the idea that they were under the ideological sway of capital. The central claim of this tendency is that capitalism is unjust, and unequal. These problems should be addressed through taxation and spending. Politics from this perspective is a matter of redistributing surplus produced in the private economy so as to make society fairer. Pushed to its most radical extreme, the logic of this argument enthrones simple commodity production as an ideal—for what, after all, could be fairer and more just than that? After payment of all the various redistributions and reparations, the payment to the working class of the "undiminished return from labor," something very close to the C-M-C circuit would emerge. The problems of this view, which for clarity's sake I am developing to its logical extreme and not presenting as it is actually argued, are perhaps well known but worth restating. Given the organizational forms, productive processes, and technical marvels that capitalism has created, breaking up and dispersing them would be utterly reactionary. The point must rather be to redeploy this already existing social power for new purposes: public ones, obviously, rather than private ones. It is absolutely essential, in short, to recognize that capitalism can in no way be described only as an "unfair" or "unjust" system; it is also a system of social production of historically unprecedented complexity and scope. But to grasp this fact, and its political meaning—which must be the subject of subsequent notes—requires quite precisely a break with petit bourgeois ideology; a break with the immediate point of view that sees capitalism through the spectacles of C-M-C.

60

Land to the people. The debate over the payment of reparations to the descendants of the enslaved often takes the form of an opposition between those emphasizing the specificity of racial injustice and those advocating a class strategy. It might be worth emphasizing in regard to this discussion that the concept of reparations itself embodies a class standpoint, if not in a sociological, certainly in an epistemological sense. For what is to be "repaired" is an injustice, suffered by a specific race. Economically, this injustice is grasped as an enormous transfer of unpaid labor to "American society." This debt has never been settled, and in fact has been exacerbated through the experience of sharecropping and then, at a later date, exclusion from the mortgage market. In sum, one could say that African Americans are owed reparations because, as a people, they have been repeatedly denied the opportunity to become petit bourgeois, unlike, presumably, their counterparts in the white working class.

There are two serious problems with this analysis. First, without in any way denying the specific horrors of slavery, it should be obvious enough that slave exploitation was not the only, or even the main, source of surplus for the US dominant class. (All the attempts to argue that slavery was somehow a precondition for US industrialization collapse under inspection. To just pose the most obvious question, if slavery was such a boon to industry, why was the US South so woefully behind the North up until at least the mid-twentieth century?) Was wage labor not also exploited, or do the advocates of reparations hold the view that the value of labor power (the wage) is equal to the value of the product of laboring? Presumably they do not; but whence, then, the special claim to reparations? (Perhaps it is a claim based on some aspects of slavery other than its unpaid character, except that estimates of the value of wealth produced by slaves play a prominent role in the discussion.) The second problem with the demand for reparations is its cryptoconservative character. In fairness it is not entirely certain what the term "reparations" means: in some cases, it seems to refer to targeted social assistance of various kinds, in others a specific cash award. But generally, the project seems to be one of petit-bourgeoisification: promotion of

homeownership, wealth accumulation, and business formation. This is about as radical as the Stolypin reforms, and if
the policy were implemented it would throw up even further
obstacles to the already beleaguered US left.

61

No social democrats here. The passage of the American
Rescue Plan carries many important lessons. First and
foremost is that a willingness to engage in massive deficit
spending is no indicator whatsoever of social democracy,
either as a policy program or as a political force. This should
already have been obvious from the even larger CARES
Act; but the point is clearer from the recent bill, since it
does substantially more to help the underlying population,
but is hardly the product of social democratic pressure; its
main exponents are neoliberal politicians recently converted
to some new form of economic nationalism. Especially
remarkable is the child tax credit, which will function as
a quasi-guaranteed income to families with children. But
key priorities of the democratic socialist left were of course
deleted: no minimum wage increase and no strengthening
of collective bargaining.

The second lesson is the substantial room the Democratic Party center has to cement its coalition exclusively
with debt; tax increases are nowhere to be found. Paradoxically, this fiscal space is a consequence of the weakness
and fragility of the world economy. It is not yet clear what
the exact limits to such a policy might be. Presumably, any
serious move to establish a guaranteed basic income on a
broad scale would create resistance, as it would tighten
labor markets; however, since so little capital is now interested in investment, this limit may be rather soft. The second
problem, and clearly the big worry for the Biden administration, is inflation. This poses a direct threat to creditors

and would provoke a sharp reaction were it to spike. The hope is clearly that by pursuing a policy of easy money and deficit spending the administration can juice the economy at least through 2022. Meanwhile, inequality increases and real growth is nowhere on the horizon. This all bears about the same relation to Keynesianism as Napoleon did to Alexander the Great.

62

The politics of class. The basic conceptual reflex of political sociology is the "search for social bases." But what if the actual connection between "isms" and their supporters is quite different? Take, for example, the relationship between socialism and the working class. There is an important sense in which the working class can only appear as a self-aware collective actor in the context of a political struggle for the establishment of postcapitalism. No socialist movement, no working class as collective actor. Of course, socialism did not create workers; industrial capitalism did that. Nevertheless, there is a very intimate link between understanding oneself as a member of a class of workers and the adoption of socialist politics such that the self-understanding virtually implies the politics.

What, then, of the substantial evidence of worker support for parties of the right in the current moment? It is perhaps a bit of lazy positivism to describe the base of the Lega Nord, or Trump's support in the rustbelt, or support for Brexit in northern England, as "working class" (ex–working class might be a better designation). It would be more precise to say that these are current or former employees in manufacturing industries whose self-understanding is predominantly regional, or national, or racial. Such groups can be described as "working class" only from the point of view of the analyst or observer, which of course means that in an important way they are not working class, only incipiently or possibly such.

This perhaps obvious set of remarks also has important implications for the understanding of identities as the result of an intersection among several structures: white workers, Black workers, and so on. As my previous notes suggested, but did not fully explain, the problem is badly posed. It is largely (although not entirely) incorrect to think of the different bases of "identity" as combining or "intersecting"; they are instead, to a degree, alternatives to one another, at least in the sphere of politics. The reason is banal. There is simply not sufficient "time in the day" to act politically on the basis of all the innumerable ways one might. Thus, the first stage is a struggle, and far from an even one at that, over the possible identities—or to use Althusser's expression, which seems helpful here, "interpolations"—through which one will act politically. The preliminary task of a socialist politics is therefore to decrease the costs of acting politically in class ways. The dominant politico-ideological system could be understood precisely as levying a tax on class politics, making alternatives to class politics appear relatively cheaper and more accessible.

63

Consolation prize. The problem of democracy remains unresolved. Up until the seventies it could be posed, as Bobbio in fact posed it, as a simple two-by-two table. Four types of modern society were conceivable: authoritarian capitalist, democratic capitalist, authoritarian socialist, and democratic socialist. While the last cell remained depressingly empty, the other three had important historical and contemporary examples. After the crisis of the dictatorships in Iberia and South America, and then even more severely with the collapse of the Soviet Union, the convergence on the democratic capitalist type seemed inexorable. (Asia of course remained a massive exception to this scheme.) The moment of Fukuyama had arrived. There seemed to be an undeniable internal relationship between capitalism and democracy.

How did the left react? In two main ways. There were many who pointed out that although capitalist democracy had won, it appeared to be getting less democratic, as parties withered and voters withdrew. This also went hand in hand with a more historical thesis: that capitalist democracy had always been based on a quiescent populace. The Latin American transitions, in which democracies had followed harsh dictatorships of the right that disciplined and pacified the working class, seemed virtually pure cases of this process; but European fascism's disciplining function was similar, as was arguably the Progressive Era with its various moral panics in the United States. The other response moved in exactly the opposite direction: it claimed that whatever democratic character modern capitalist societies had assumed was because of the working class. This second argument has become something of a new orthodoxy. It first emerged as a critique of modernization theory (Therborn). It has now taken on a clearly reactionary or perhaps chloroforming significance. The thesis functions as what could be termed either "consolation prize Marxism" or "subaltern Fukuyamism." Its psychological effect is to boost the morale of social democrats of various hues by providing them with an uplifting narrative in which industrial workers, or sometimes just "ordinary people," achieve democratic rights against the resistance of powerful reactionary forces. The facts of how the suffrage was actually extended usually through reforms spearheaded by reactionary or at least quite conservative politicians (Bismarck, Disraeli, Napoleon III, Giolitti) rarely get in the way of this morality tale; that it performs what Merton would have termed a "latent function" is suggested by the mass, length, and pseudorigor of the books and articles devoted to sustaining it. The function is to integrate scholars who would otherwise produce more hard-hitting and critical work, but who are now bogged down in indefensible positions.

It must be said, however, that neither of the two responses to the Fukuyama moment has really adequately dealt with the democracy problem. To pose the issue correctly requires a break with the metaphysics of sovereignty. It is important to recognize how right Weber was when he said that "the people" do not rule in modern states, regardless of whatever theory of sovereignty predominates in them. (Mosca, who is often wrongly dismissed as failing to understand democracy, of course made a similar point.) It's also never sufficiently emphasized that Weber's types of legitimate authority make no mention of democracy. They speak instead of legal-rational authority. The Althusserians would say, I suppose, that this is a "symptomatic" silence.

What perhaps should be recognized here is Weber's total, if implicit, convergence with Lenin on precisely this point: both of them saw the terms "democracy" and "state" as antithetical, and quite rightly so. (It is true that Weber expressed himself somewhat differently than Lenin, but he was quite clear that the "people" never rule in the modern state.) How does one abolish an antithesis? By rendering it impossible. To imagine a postcapitalist political order is to imagine an order without sovereignty—and therefore without the metaphysics of sovereignty and its terminology, such as "democracy"—but with coordination and rationality. Surprising as it may seem, the Hayekian phrase, from *The Fatal Conceit*, "the extended order of human cooperation" somehow gets at the idea much more effectively than the limp and trite expression "socialist democracy," which carries with it both a legacy of defeat and the faint odor of metaphysical decay.

64

Metaracism. A new form of racism has been identified; it
will have a long and convoluted subsequent development,
especially when the lawyers figure it out. A story in the local
paper described calls for the resignation of the vice presi-
dent of the San Francisco school board after the discovery
of tweets that displayed an anti-Asian bias. The paradox is
that the posts themselves were mostly claims that "Asians"
tend to embrace the ideology of white supremacy—in short
that they are racist as a group. The article, with no irony at
all, referred to them as "racist tweets." What is most interesting, and bizarre, about the whole affair is its implication
that the meaning of the term "racism" has shifted. The word
no longer means only the expression of disdain for a given
ethnic group; it also includes accusations that one group
may tend to act in racist ways toward another group. Thus,
the accusation of racism itself may be a form of racism. This
is the idea of metaracism; and given the byzantine absurdi-
ties of American ethno-politics, it is a tool likely to serve
many masters.

65

Lessons to be drawn. The fascism industry is booming.
Scholars who have devoted their careers to an intense and
horrible, but certainly well delimited, historical period have
suddenly emerged with lessons: about masculinity, the truth,
institutions, and so forth. The effect is like a collage: black-
and-white pictures of Mussolini and Hitler pasted next to
images of Modi, Bolsonaro, and of course the inevitable
ex–reality TV star. But all this explanatory energy and
analogizing is misdirected. For why would the rise of brutal
ignoramuses to positions of authority surprise anyone in a

capitalist society? The real puzzle has always been quite different: the perdurance of the strange simulacrum of popular
authority that passes for democracy in the rich and not-so-
rich world, as well as the occasional emergence of leaders
of real quality and substance (De Gaulle perhaps above all).

66

Canonizing. Sociology is apparently in the process of
decolonizing itself. As I suggested in note 54, this is in part
an academic-bureaucratic project with syllabus revision,
edited volumes, and new targets of canonization on the
horizon. A strong point of the project is the recognition
that sociology emerged during the age of imperialism and
that this fact gave the field a cosmopolitan and comparative
ambition lost after the Parsonsian synthesis, which was both
grand and a bit boring. The weakness of the decolonizers
lies in their deadening approach to ideas. For the enthusiasts
of this project, such as the Australian sociologist Raewyn
Connell, for example, the elevation of Durkheim and Weber
(then joined at a later period by Marx) to the status of
classics is the result of translations, edited volumes, and
curricula, and not of any intrinsic power of the work. In
the past, per Connell, there were different figures such as
Spencer, Comte, and Martineau. In the future there might
be new ones.

Undoubtedly there is considerable truth in all this, but
what the decolonizers never get around to is the analysis
of ideas. Why is this? It is connected to a cluster of epistemological and ontological assumptions shared across
sociology, from the most ardent exponents of postcolonial-
ism to hardcore positivists. It could be called the dogma of
the shapeless flux. Its picture of intellectual history is something like this: There exists a massive body of texts with
ideas and theories of more or less equal quality (Connell

equates Sumner's "folkways" to Weber's sociology of religion and Comte's theory of progress to Hegel's philosophy of history, for example). Some of these texts are arbitrarily elevated to the status of must-reads because their study serves some latent function for sociology, such as reinforcing professional pride and presumably also the interests of the white middle-class men who embody it. Occasionally the time comes to shake up the texts; this is an especially urgent task in the current period because of the need to diversify in demographic terms the voices in the curriculum. Without falling into a lazy traditionalism, it should be obvious that this set of protocols for understanding the history of sociology is guaranteed to produce nothing but cynicism, both concerning the previous canon and whatever new candidates are forthcoming. What it forgets is that the first step in an analysis is the critique and reconstruction of the ideas. Whatever one might say about Parsons's *Structure of Social Action*, at least he got this starting point right. The decolonizers, in contrast, are producing nothing more than more or less extensive annotated bibliographies.

67

The rumpled blanket. It is very difficult to break with the flat, linear conception of time that so dominates contemporary civilization. Interestingly, though, the world of the digital image and social media profile violates this conception daily. Events in the past, even in the preonline past, can be suddenly forced into the present; iPhoto, Facebook, and Instagram algorithms regularly prompt "memories" by sending images that provoke a flood of half-buried emotions: happiness, longing, regret. It is not just images; it is also texts. The availability of a huge swath of the corpus of human knowledge in multiple languages has two quite contradictory potential effects. The first is a sensation of the arbitrariness of all intellectual traditions. In this sense there might be a subterranean connection between the exponentially increasing availability of scanned texts and the ontology of the "shapeless flux" and its associated project of syllabus revision discussed in the previous note. The second possibility is quite the opposite: the establishment of a much stronger and deeper connection to intellectual traditions. (It is dizzying to realize, for example, what a huge trove of the history of left thought is available through the *New Left Review* archive to anyone with a decent internet connection.) A paradoxical feature of the massive availability of texts is that, because of copyright restrictions, texts produced before 1923 are much more readily accessible than those produced after. Thus, the intellectual world of the late nineteenth and early twentieth centuries has never been more accessible than it is at the present moment. (This very much includes the moment of the late nineteenth and early twentieth centuries themselves.) In contrast, the intellectual world that runs from roughly 1924 to 1994 or so is relatively more difficult to access. This is another example of the nonlinearity of historical time, which would be better thought of as a rumpled blanket with peaks and valleys than as a sheet stretching flat and featureless in every direction.

68

Problem shifts. What happened to the petite bourgeoisie? From the 1890s to the 1980s, defining the class character of small-scale owners of property and various more or less credentialed workers was perhaps the central problem of class analysis. Now, however, it is all workers versus capital. It is hardly the case that the petite bourgeoisie has diminished in significance. The relentless demand for college degrees shows as much. Indeed, there is a good case to be made that this is the stratum that continues to produce the basic ideological legitimations of contemporary class society, even in its "political capitalist" phase, believing, as it does, most sincerely in the theodicy of merit and education. But the analysis of the class is completely absent from discussions on the US left at least. There are three reasons for this.

First, more than any other Marxian class category, the petite bourgeoisie exists exclusively as a category of analysis, never a category of practice or self-identification. One might happily join the working class and struggle against the capitalists; no one ever wants to be petit bourgeois (least of all those who are actually such). Second, any close analysis of the class raises political difficulties since it disturbs the posited unity of the working class. Striking schoolteachers and nurses are to be called workers; to describe them as petit bourgeois violates one of the basic dogmas of the contemporary social democratic left: that the working class makes up the vast majority of the population, and that only a retrograde fetishization of manufacturing could blind one to this obvious fact. The third reason is the present weakness of Marxism as a theoretical tradition. Strong traditions openly identify and seek to resolve anomalies, which in the case of Marxism are always also political problems. Weak or degenerating traditions hide their anomalies with verbal legerdemain. The deletion of the petite bourgeoisie as a category, together with an overly expansive definition of the working class, is a classic example of such a move. One sign of a true revitalization of Marxism would be the reemergence of the petite bourgeoisie as a central theoretical and empirical object. This is obviously a political task as well. For identifying the real interests of petty proprietors and the credentialed is of course one precondition for mobilizing the group into a coalition with the producers of surplus value as more conventionally understood.

69

The cultural logic of late Kautskyism. The new literature on socialism (Robinson and Sunkara, for example) compares with the neo-Marxism of the seventies and eighties in a way that recalls Gramsci's contrast of Renaissance and Reformation—itself a coded reference to the contrast between Marx and Engels and their Second International epigones, as well as the hapless Bukharin. Gramsci suggested that all great cultural and political movements go through two phases: a phase of Renaissance that is sophisticated and rigorous, but restricted to an intellectual elite, and a phase of Reformation in which the doctrine is simplified but made more accessible. It is in this second phase that the theory grips the masses and becomes "myth," in the Sorelian sense. Are we living through a period of Reformation (or Second Internationalization)? There are many differences between the contemporary period of popularization and its original in the 1890s. The first difference is the lack of a real working-class audience. *Jacobin*, very much by its own admission, is a publication aimed at graduate students and recent PhDs. The second difference is the cultural style of the new socialist literature. In total contrast to the poignant sincerity of Kautsky's best writing, for example, a rather ironic tone hangs over the products of the DSA intelligentsia. *Jacobin*'s colorful images, self-deprecating responses to social media attacks, and tongue-in-cheek section headings ("Means of Deduction," "Cultural Capital") exemplify a cultural style that could be called "postmodern Kautskyism" or "Kautskyism in an ironic mode." Like its forebear, it is characterized by the tendency to cover up and slur over theoretical and political difficulties; but unlike the original, this is all done with a nod and a wink.

70

Slow learner. I am learning many lessons, but the most important ones concern time. The whole organization of time under capitalism discounts and ignores the now; everything is organized in relation to an ever receding past and a projected future. The present becomes a mere means of linking the two voids. This relationship to time is always violent and irrational. But in my current circumstances it is pathological as well. One careens from painful nostalgia to despair without realizing what is happening now, which is precisely everything.

71

Today and tomorrow. The most striking thing about what I have termed the "dogma of the shapeless flux" is how profoundly incompatible it is with many very ordinary experiences. Consider the problem of periods or epochs. There is a general, if highly inconsistent, skepticism of periodization in contemporary social thought. Jameson pointed out some years ago that temporal metaphors of transitions from feudalism to capitalism or from traditional to modern society were being replaced by the spatial metaphor of globalization. Now in some ways the two things have merged in the numerous global histories of capitalism that have appeared; but the recurrence of "capitalism talk" has come with a vagueness about what exactly capitalism is as a historical period, so that this recurrence, too, partakes of the skepticism of periodization instanced by globalization.

But does anyone doubt that "the life-course" has definite periods? Children do not become adults gradually, year by year, as they accumulate experiences and competencies. Instead, what happens is that at one moment they are children who need support, guidance, and advice, and the next moment, after a brief and poignant period called adolescence, they are adults who are giving support, guidance, and advice. The change is sudden, total, and irrevocable. One suspects that it is often precipitated by a trauma that suddenly crystallizes what had existed previously only in a latent or suspended state. Given this highly general experience (the substantial cross-cultural variation concerns mostly the age at which this occurs for different genders), why is there so much skepticism about periods and epochs in history? Is it that people think that what holds for the biological individual cannot be applied to society as a whole? But the skepticism is unfounded. If individuals can experience sudden, qualitative changes, why can't the social relations in which they are enmeshed, and which they help to create? The hypothesis of the existence of qualitatively distinct periods seems at least more reasonable than its denial.

72

Dialectics on the cheap. Why are so many historians now committed to describing commodity production in the slave South and Latin America as "capitalist"? The trend is obvious: books and dissertations dedicated to showing how slave owners used double-entry bookkeeping and were deeply enmeshed in credit markets. The limited theoretical relevance of much of this work is equally obvious. As Weber pointed out over a century ago, highly developed networks of commodity production are entirely compatible with an economic dynamic fundamentally different from modern rational capitalism with free wage labor. But as an academic strategy, calling cash-crop production using slavery "capitalist" comes with some very obvious benefits. It allows the scholar in question to enjoy the profits of

radicalism, particularly by revealing that many major Wall
Street firms and London financial houses made money off
slavery, while avoiding the far less acceptable task of dealing
with the existence of exploitation even in the freest of free
labor markets. Indeed, perversely, the Marxian critique can
be presented as "conservative" precisely because it fails to
recognize the slave underbelly of free wage labor. But this
is a cheap sort of dialectics, since it fails to register that
Marx's critique of capitalism was radical precisely because
it made the heroic assumption, never meant to be descrip-
tively accurate, that labor power was free and paid at its
value. Even in this "Eden of the rights of man," the engine
of exploitation and accumulation was at work in the hidden
abode of production.

73

Music class. What is a class? The metaphors normally
deployed to describe classes ("group," "position," "location,"
"status") are not particularly apt. Perhaps a better one
would be "ensemble," a term that should be understood in
the sense of a musical ensemble. Such structures (quartets,
trios, orchestras) can best be described as "antagonistically
cooperative." They are cooperative in the sense that the
players must work precisely for the production of a common
product and each must fulfill a precisely defined role. But
ensembles are rife with antagonism; different players have
different levels of skill, different styles, different internal
senses of time. Strong charismatic players will impose
their own visions on the group: sometimes to good effect,
sometimes to ill.

Furthermore, there is a subculture associated with each
instrument. Violin players are as a rule highly individualistic and committed to virtuosity for its own sake. There are
lots of them in an orchestra, so they are divided into two

sections (firsts and seconds). Within this hierarchy there is
ferocious struggle among the individual players. Cellos are
in general more cooperative; there are fewer of them, and
they have a quasi-proletarian function within the orchestra,
supporting the "superstructure" of the melodic line carried
by the first violins. Since at least Casals, Rostropovich,
Shafran, and Feuermann, the cello, too, has its *virtuosi*;
but it is still the workhorse of the orchestra. Violas occupy
an ambiguous and slightly suspect role. There are few of
them, and they tend to be the target of jokes by the players
of the other sections. There is a whole tedious repertoire
of viola jokes, the basic point of which is always that viola
players are really violin players who have found a rather
favorable niche with lower levels of competition. (As with
everything else in the United States, these differences are
ethnically marked. In youth orchestras the violin sections
tend to be heavily dominated by Chinese American kids, the
cello section tends to be a rather mixed bag, and the violas
are the province of the Russian and Jewish kids.)

The ensemble, then, is a highly complex structure of solidarity. If a class is an ensemble too, of a very different sort,
the process of its formation could be imagined as analogous to the transition from the cacophony of the individual
players as they tune to the performance of an orchestra or
chamber group. What then is the role of the party in relation
to the ensemble? The party is the conductor, whose job is
to coordinate the individual performances not by fostering
a "group consciousness" but by encouraging the players to
listen to the other parts and mutually adjust their voices.
Class consciousness would be the awareness of one's role in
a common project; not, then, an inert sense of "belonging,"
but a structured, active awareness of existing for something. One might think that this metaphor has authoritarian
implications because of its reliance on the conductor as a
central figure. But this is to misunderstand the conductor's
role; conductors are persuaders who encourage the mutual

orientation of the musicians to one another's performances. And, of course, in smaller chamber groups there is no conductor; the ensemble "conducts" itself.

74

Magic kingdom. One common interpretation of contemporary politics counterposes highly educated urban dwellers who live in a world of reason and tolerance to a group of rural and exurban rubes mentally trapped in the Middle Ages and victimized by hucksters of various sorts. This seriously underestimates the extent of magical thinking among the "professional managerial class" itself. A very thin membrane separates the kombucha-drinking, vaccine-skeptical exercise enthusiasts who are a dime a dozen in California's coastal cities from the QAnon maniacs who have suddenly achieved such notoriety. That the culture of the coastal New Age is uncomfortably close to the most unhinged right-wing conspiracy nuts was dramatically underlined by the Q Shaman: a vegan failed actor. It was also demonstrated by the recent story of a grade school teacher from San Clemente (Nixon's old stomping ground) who was filmed participating in the political Bacchanalia of January 6.

Apparently, she had no particular political convictions until Covid restrictions hit. This was the catalyst for her new husband, described as a "yoga guru" who specialized in "'sound healing' with gongs, Tibetan bowls and Aboriginal didgeridoos," to found an antivaccination right-wing group called the American Phoenix Project.[*] The teacher, following her soulmate, then embraced QAnon and a variety of other bizarre conspiracy theories that landed her finally among the Jeffersonian throngs on the steps of the Capitol. This is

---

[*]   Matthew Rosenberg, "A Teacher Marched to the Capitol. When She Got Home, the Fight Began," *New York Times*, April 10, 2021.

just an extreme version of a very common experience for anyone who lives in the Golden State: the slightly "crunchy" or "hipster" friend who suddenly reveals herself as an antivaxxer despite the otherwise respectable exterior and apparent cognitive normality. What makes these transitions possible is the perspective its adherents have in common: a basically magical worldview that can appear either in the form of secularized mysticism or belief in the existence of a nefarious cabal that controls the political scene. In general, this is another indicator of how superficial the phenomenon of "rationalization" is in contemporary capitalism. One suspects that only a thin layer lives in the disenchanted world of instrumental rationality, means-ends relationships, and goal-oriented activity. Outside of this circle is a world of ritual, magic, and occult powers.

75

Blankets. In crochet there is a technique called "granny squares," in which the maker produces a number of small multicolored squares of yarn. These are subsequently assembled to form a blanket. The technique is often deployed to use up odds and ends of yarn accumulated as leftovers from previous projects. Emanuela recently completed a very beautiful such blanket. These notes are also "granny squares." They are scraps of thought worked up into little tiles. But whether they will form a striking mosaic will depend on how they are arranged and put together.

76

Progressive Burke. Why Polanyi? It is hard to deny the enormous popularity of the Hungarian émigré among self-described left-wing sociologists. But what is being offered?

A clever vocabulary ("fictitious commodities," "double movement," "disembedding") and some insights about the contradictions of the commodity form. It is difficult to see a strong explanatory agenda deriving from *The Great Transformation*, for example. There is little to no theory of capitalist development, and the political sociology is highly abstract and mechanical. As is often the case with intellectual trends, Polanyi's current popularity is best understood as the expression of the social position of the intelligentsia. What does Polanyi offer here?

Above all, relevance. With Polanyi one can be critical of capitalism, or at least critical of markets (property plays little analytical role in Polanyi's theory) without being a Marxist. Polanyi also offers optimism. For the political point is always to establish a coalition among various social groups interested in protecting "society" from "the market." Furthermore, "marketization" always generates counter-movements, so the task of the intelligentsia is to influence their direction. In this scheme there is no need to worry about the etiolation of the working class as a coherent actor: there is always a countermovement just around the corner. What is most striking about Polanyism, however, is its conservative timidity. Politics, in the Polanyian mode, is always a matter of protection, defense, reembedding. Tacitly abandoned of course is the idea of a new order. In this way Polanyism connects to the concept of social justice, which also conceives of all social movements as attempts at "harm repair" or "restoration." In all this there is more Burke than Marx.

77

Evergreen Hungarian. Explaining the popularity of Polanyi may require several further notes. Consider the debate between Lachner (a self-styled "hard Polanyian") and Block and Somers in the recent issue of *Theory and Society*. The fundamental question separating them is whether Polanyi was a non-Marxist revolutionary socialist or a non-Marxist social democrat. Lacher argues the former, Block and Somers the latter. In terms of the textual evidence there seems to be little doubt that Lacher has the better argument. Evidently, Polanyi hated social democracy. Block and Somers, as is their wont, press Polanyi into the service of their mealy-mouthed politics with little concern for textual or historical accuracy. But the Block and Somers interpretation, that Polanyi saw capitalist economies as always shot through with state intervention, reflects a certain truth about neoliberalism. The point could be put this way. Block and Somers are right to emphasize that neoliberalism is fundamentally a political project: a program of upward redistribution. But they are absolutely wrong in projecting this back onto the entire history of capitalism. This reveals only their inability to think historically about capitalism as a system of exploitation, and more particularly their inability to grasp the specificity of its current political-capitalist phase (since they describe all phases of capitalism as "embedded" politically).

78

Jacobins. Intellectually, we live in the age of "adjectival capitalism." In the nineties of course it was varieties of capitalism, then in the 2000s "neoliberal capitalism," and now the emergence or spread of "racial capitalism," a term initially put into circulation in the United States in the early eighties by Cedric Robinson, but widely popular only recently. This reflects the profound political weakness of the left in the current period. It is as if the critique of the wage labor–capital relation required a supplement to give it teeth. Capitalism is to be condemned because it has always gone hand in hand with other oppressions: racial, gender, national. But the irrationality of capitalism as a system of production and surplus allocation, its inhuman counterfinality, is somehow insufficient as a critique. Why is this the case? It might be connected with the new phase of capitalism (what I have termed "political capitalism": another adjectival form). It might be the case that the political supports of surplus extraction are now so obvious that the critique of capitalism necessarily takes on a naive quasi-enlightenment form. Who needs a critical theory to understand bank bailouts, tax cuts, and foreclosures? But it might also be the case that the new adjectival capitalism talk is simply an occult demand for a capitalism without adjectives. Or maybe all these things are true. Maybe the left today has slipped back behind the period of the modern labor movement so that its historical task really is a Jacobin one: to end the old regime and introduce the era of formal equality.

79

Political fantasy. It would be a very comforting story to imagine that Biden's strikingly ambitious domestic policy agenda (oversold by the liberal media but nonetheless remarkable) has something to do with pressure from the Democratic Party's neo-social-democratic left. This is a fantasy. If the Squad and DSA did not exist, Biden's policies would be closely similar to what he is offering now, for simple electoral reasons. The real pathbreaker for the Biden agenda is Trump, who destroyed neoliberalism as a distinctive intellectual and political force. (Note well: Biden's immigration and tariff policies have changed very little from the Trump years.) Abundantly endowed with the low cunning of a business ignoramus, Trump instinctively grasped the truth that the idea of a free market managed by technocrats was a pile of nonsense. Biden is the beneficiary of this insight. Where is Larry Summers? Grumbling about inflation, but for the moment ignored. None of this is imaginable without the intellectual wrecking ball that swung so wildly over the last four years.

80

The state and strategy. The Marxist "debate on the state," which unfolded from the late sixties to the late seventies, is riven with paradox and reversal. These developments can best be grasped by posing the question of the relationship between political tactics and analyses of the state. The roots of the discussion go back to debates within the First International concerning the notion of the "dictatorship of the proletariat." The problem here is whether the state as an institution has a class character. Marx's point regarding the civil wars in France was that the bourgeois state is a class institution; thus, the proletariat must create a new type of state. The revolutionary process then required a specific phase or transitional period during which the preexisting apparatus would be dismantled and replaced, leading to a structurally new relationship between state and society.

Kautsky proposed a new account. In his clash with Trotsky and Lenin—although the idea was already implicit in his earlier work—he developed the notion of the state as an institution that had no particular class character. Like technology or science, it could be taken up and deployed for a variety of uses and certainly need not be "smashed"; indeed, such a smashing, for Kautsky, would be a form of political Luddism. Lenin, on the contrary, defended the revolutionary Marxist view that the bourgeois state possessed a class character in its institutional set-up.

And so the debate stood until the late sixties, when it reemerged with the Poulantzas-Miliband exchange. In this exchange Poulantzas developed a basically Leninist analysis, suggesting that the state was a class state institutionally (or structurally). Although the empirical focus of the argument differed, Anderson's *Lineages of the Absolutist State* made a similar claim for the late feudal state. The basic thrust of this line of argument was that the class character of the state should be grasped in institutional rather than interpersonal terms; such analyses were also clearly revolutionary in their political implications. Thus, by around the mid-seventies, the following set of associations could be made: Structuralism/Revolutionary Marxism, Instrumentalism/Left Social Democracy. These associations between type of analysis and type of politics were broken apart in the late seventies. The crucial turning point here was Fred Block's essay "The Ruling Class Does Not Rule." Block claimed that the capitalist character of the state was the consequence of the division of labor between state managers and capitalists. State managers want to promote capitalist growth because growth is the main condition for expanding employment and tax revenue and thus fiscal means and political support. Therefore, all else being equal, state managers will seek to secure business confidence regardless of whatever other beliefs they might hold. Block held this theory to be even more structural and less interpersonal than Poulantzas's. But what of the dictatorship of the proletariat, the decisive problem of Marxist state theory, as Therborn indicated? Block was totally silent on this issue, and what his article in fact achieved was the linking together for the first time of a structural theory of the capitalist state with a social democratic politics (even if the latter was somewhat disguised by revolutionary phraseology). If one wanted to take up the question anew, the starting point would be the conditions that produce a division of labor between those who live "off and for politics" (Weber) and those instead whose full-time activity is more or less in the realm of the economy. The dictatorship of the proletariat could then be specified as the overcoming of this division of labor; but that is basically the meaning of smashing the state.

81

False friends. Two forms of Bourdieusianism dominate contemporary social thought. The first is a rather skeptical and apolitical rightist form that contents itself with describing the operations of "symbolic power." The second is a more engaged form that seeks to actively reconstruct the social world by recategorizing groups within it. Individuals may pass from one form to the other over the course of their intellectual/political lives, as Bourdieu himself did. These transformations have created a great deal of confusion, especially on the US left, not least because there is a rather substantial group of left Bourdieusians writing about various topics familiar to the Marxist tradition: the state, imperialism, racism, and sometimes, although less consistently, capitalism. Thus, giants on the Anglo-American left, such as Mike Davis, Adolph Reed Jr., or more elaborately Michael Burawoy, have tried to establish a sort of détente with the left Bourdieusians who offer, they imagine, a sophisticated way of thinking about society. It should be emphasized, in this regard, that the basic ontological commitments of Bourdieusians, of whatever stripe, are incompatible with any rational materialism and ultimately with science as such. The best example of this comes from the topic where it would seem that the Bourdieusians have the most to contribute: race. Race, we all know, is "constructed." So far, so banal. But, and this is the decisive point, Bourdieusians always describe the process of racial construction as a matter of classification. In doing so they reveal their basically neo-Kantian view, a position they come by honestly through Durkheim. (Bourdieu is very much Durkheim's heir; his supposed synthesis of classical theory is massively skewed toward his fellow countryman.)

It must be emphasized that to say that race is "constructed" does not, and should not, imply that racial formation is primarily a matter of classification. Such a view both hopelessly narrows the explanatory problem and violates the reality of racial formations, which are far more than classifications. For such formations are often formed by highly robust material interests—as when, for example, white homeowners were quite rationally worried about the declining value of their houses when Blacks moved into white working-class neighborhoods in American cities in the seventies. That is to say, there are numerous historical circumstances in which it makes a great deal of sense for people to act collectively as races, thereby both reproducing and transforming racial formations. Nevertheless, it would be correct to say that races do not exist in the way that racial ideologies say they do. They are instead to be understood as phenomena that allude to the underlying structure: the class structure. (Of course, phenomena are real; but they are not real in the same kind of way that structures are. This is the whole difficulty.)

But if racial formation is reduced to a matter of classification, the races become again inexplicable. For the question that no Bourdieusian neo-Kantian ever poses is, precisely why—that is, under what historical circumstances—would the classification of groups assume a racial form? The answer cannot be to refer to the classification, because that would be a tautology. But it is precisely here that Bourdieusians, and particularly the left-wing variety, end up; thus, their enormous enthusiasm for studying censuses, a task that they invest with a metaphysical enthusiasm inexplicable outside their particular social ontology.

82

Cages. The project of postcolonial sociology often seems self-contradictory. Consider the following excerpt from a programmatic article published in *Contemporary Sociology* in 2018 by Raewyn Connell:

> Mainstream knowledge formation, generally speaking, works on the assumption that there is one and only one episteme ... There is a certain grandeur in this conception: one social science that can work for all humanity. But there are stark problems, too. It violates just about everything we know in the sociology of knowledge. It's inconsistent with the experience of cross-cultural encounter. And because there is really only one body of social thought in a position to act globally as The One, in practice this epistemology provides an alibi for Eurocentrism.
>
> Many people, therefore, have opted for a mosaic epistemology. In this conception, separate knowledge systems sit beside each other like tiles in a mosaic, each based on a specific culture or historical experience. Most indigenous knowledge projects seem to presume a local, at most a regional, validity. Mosaic epistemology offers a clear alternative to northern hegemony and global inequality, replacing the priority of one knowledge system with respectful relations among many.[*]

It is not clear to what extent Connell herself entirely adopts this conception, as she subsequently goes on to offer metaphors other than mosaics, such as the "braiding of knowledge projects." But these are minor matters. What is remarkable is the contradiction between the claim

---

[*] Raewyn Connell, "Decolonizing Sociology," *Contemporary Sociology* 47, no. 4 (2018): 403–4.

that there in fact exist multiple "knowledge projects" and the statement that any assertion of a single episteme "provides an alibi for Eurocentrism," to be avoided at all costs. The problem is this: the claim that there exist multiple epistemologies or "epistemes," whether they be "tiled" or "braided" or whatever else, is itself a universal claim about knowledge. From what perspective do these varied epistemologies or "knowledge projects" become visible? What episteme justifies the idea that there are multiple epistemes?

Here Connell falls into flat empiricism. She states that the position claiming only a single episteme is empirically false ("violates just about everything we know in the sociology of knowledge"). Thus, she seems to say that it is an incontrovertible fact that there exist multiple epistemes. But doesn't such a claim simply reinstate what had just been dethroned: a universal statement of fact, not only applicable across epistemes, but that has the existence of the number of epistemes as its content? To put the point differently, wouldn't it be more consistent to claim that the existence of either single or multiple epistemes itself depends on the episteme, or better, the meta-episteme within which one is operating? This terrain is, in a sense, very well plowed; the contradiction described has obviously dogged the Foucauldian project from the beginning, and it is hard to see postcolonial sociology as much more than a very late retreading of these paths. To avoid these conundrums, it is necessary to locate their source, and that is the very idea of an episteme or "knowledge system." For there is really no reason to regard knowers as inherently trapped in frameworks, languages, or other more or less elaborate and restrictive cages. The question of knowledge is not a question of epistemes, but a question of praxis and its rational comprehension.

83

Imagination. What explains the apparently widespread interest in UFOs among US politicos? The curiosity is entirely bipartisan, according to an extensive recent article in the *New Yorker*: Reid, Rubio, Obama, and the ubiquitous Leon Panetta are all apparently more or less enthusiastic ufologists.* In June of this year a report from the Unidentified Aerial Phenomena Task Force is due out. This document is being produced particularly at Rubio's urging: the senator inserted language into the Intelligence Authorization Act to request that the Secretary of Defense produce it. What does this mean? One hypothesis is that the enthusiasm is the expression of a distorted or displaced utopian impulse, an impulse that is as necessary for the reproduction of the established order as it is for its potential transformation. Obviously, the universalization of capitalism has created a sort of crisis of legitimacy in this sense. It is easier to imagine an alien civilization with technology thousands or millions of years in advance of our own than it is to imagine a society beyond, or challenging, capitalism (especially for American politicians).

84

Dangerous characters. A profound and quite recent tectonic shift has occurred in American culture, the significance of which needs to be plumbed. The vocation of teaching is now understood on all sides of the political spectrum to be a highly dangerous and suspect profession. Texts are accorded thaumaturgical powers to harm and damage.

---

*   Gideon Lewis-Kraus, "How the Pentagon Started Taking U.F.O.s Seriously," *New Yorker*, April 30, 2021.

Syllabi containing too many dead white guys, or Marxists (the two categories often overlap) are viewed as celebratory monuments either of racial domination or past totalitarianisms. Critique is treated as violence. The underlying cause is the symbolization of ideas. These are now viewed as hypostatizations of preconstituted groups; a stance that thrusts the student into one of two dialectically linked roles: the spluttering, fanatic *enragé* or the docile worshipper. For both, ideas remain "object" or *Gegenstand* in the sense of that which is external. This-sidedness withers and cannot develop. The vocation of the teacher is reduced to that of a museum curator: either boring or offensive, depending on one's taste. How could critical rationality be expected to develop under such conditions?

85

Reactionary insight. One of the most intellectually debilitating, but also most common, errors is the confusion of progressive or revolutionary standpoints with analytic power. Consider George Fitzhugh, perhaps the most notorious social theorist in American intellectual history. Fitzhugh's claim to fame, apart from being one of the very first writers to use sociology in the title of his books, was his novel justification of slavery. Fitzhugh argued that slave-master relations formed an ideal community without the evils of the struggle for existence that characterized the "free society" of the North. Aside from denouncing the alienation and dehumanization of the market, he also developed an early critique of imperialism. The point that needs to be underlined is that Fitzhugh's critical insights into early US capitalism were inspired by his firm commitment to slavery; without that commitment he never would have had these insights. The point is easily generalized: insight is as often the product of reaction as it is the commitment to transformation. This is one reason why policing the syllabus and treating past ideas as if they were monuments is as likely to be as damaging to those committed to the humanized society as to their enemies.

86

Memories. The day was cold but bright. Scraps of snow clung to the ground in patches here and there. We took a bus (very sturdily built and well heated, as autobus production was one of Hungary's specialties under state socialism) to the end of the line on the outskirts of Buda. Eamon's stroller was virtually useless in the soaked red clay, and I think I may have had to carry him in his bassinet the last few yards up to the ugly brick arch announcing the entrance to Szoborpark: the statue park that is one of the many examples of the attempt to monetize and touristize the state socialist period evident everywhere in Eastern Europe. Having paid the entrance fee, we passed under the arch and entered a modestly sized lot around which the statues were arranged in a circle traced by a narrow path. What was immediately remarkable was how few of the supposed monuments to communism made any direct reference to the "people's democracy" that emerged after 1948. One I particularly remember was a moving tribute to partisan volunteers in the Spanish Civil War, and there were numerous others dedicated to the "struggle against fascism." Béla Kun's dictatorship, in which Lukács had been minister of culture, had a glittering chrome representation.

The politics of statuary is quite fascinating. Why is there still a giant obelisk outside the Stadio Olimpico in Rome commemorating Mussolini, while memorializations of relatively unknown antifascist Hungarian partisans are considered so tainted by "totalitarianism" that they must be hidden away? And what about the Valle de los Caídos, built by slave labor in Franco's Spain, and surely one of the most obscene monuments in all of Europe, but a well-organized tourist attraction with a constant stream of Pullmans, a gift shop, and a cafeteria associated with it? And Confederate monuments? Robert E. Lee is no longer acceptable, at least outside Gettysburg, which is a Szoborpark on a very grand scale, but why is it okay to memorialize Tecumseh Sherman, butcher of the Seminoles? And what about Curtis LeMay, beside whom many Wehrmacht commanders seem paragons of humanitarianism, but who apparently has a building named after him in Nebraska? What should always be asked about "the politics of memorialization" is, "Which monuments are considered uncontroversial, and why is that?"

87

Connecting. The effort to remain relevant is often the shortest route to history's dustbin. If the language and idea-world that a teacher uses is simply a clarified version of the student's preexisting common sense, what relevance is that to anyone? The ideas must be strange, they must be difficult, they must antagonize the student. Otherwise, they pass over the learner like a light breeze leaving her in unruffled sameness; or, to put it differently, they are irrelevant in the sense that it would not matter if she had been exposed to them or not.

88

Cheaters. Of all the adjectival capitalisms (described in note 78) currently swirling about, none seems more prevalent than "racial capitalism." It is difficult to understand what "capitalism" refers to in this expression. The focus on wage labor, to the exclusion of serfdom and slavery, is held to be a form of ethnocentric blindness. Capitalism is a "world system" linking the unfree labor of the periphery to the industrial centers of the core. This image has a long lineage: Bakunin, Lenin, Fanon, Gunder Frank, Wallerstein. Robinson elaborated the argument and emphasized the racial difference between the "white" core and the colonized world. The underlying idea of all these claims is that capitalism depends for its reproduction on a continuous transfer of surplus extracted by force from colonized or enslaved peoples. But here empirical and theoretical issues must be carefully distinguished.

It is a fact that inputs produced by coerced labor featured prominently in the Industrial Revolution (cotton is the obvious example). It is also a fact that within many national territories (Italy, the United States, and Germany, to take three examples) labor-repressive agricultural systems, in which the direct producers were invariably racialized (southerners in Italy, Blacks in the United States, Poles in Germany), coexisted with powerful industrial sectors. But this raises the question, Is the connection between unfree labor and industrial capitalism causal? Did slavery, serfdom, and other forms of labor repression make the exploitation of wage labor possible? This seems doubtful on historical grounds. Capitalism has shown a clear ability to survive both the end of slavery and formal colonialism. The reasons for this are many; for one thing, while unpaid labor may produce low-cost inputs for some capitalists, it also restricts the market for all capitalists. For another, capitalism's specific feature is the ability to lower unit costs through the adoption of new technology and organizational forms. The intensification or prolongation of the working day is unnecessary for the expansion of surplus value. What of the politics of "racial capitalism"? There are two ways these can develop: either as a radical critique of imperialism, or as a petit bourgeois demand for fair exchange. This political instability results from the fundamental concept of exploitation at work in "racial capitalism": the rip-off.

89

Burke or Robespierre. What is the real debate in comparative politics? The field sprawls across the borderlands of sociology and political science, and every few years throws up a major, or at least ambitious, work that seeks to explain either the development of the state or democracy or both. Some identify struggles over taxes as key, others develop elaborate genealogies of various institutional forms, still others emphasize culture and religion (of course, as in every other area of sociology, class analysis is in full retreat). These intellectual battles are carried on with great sound and fury, usually ranging variously specified "materialisms" (which have about as much to do with Marxism as Orange Crush has to do with Orange Juice) against either the miasma of "historical institutionalism" or culturalist arguments pitched at various levels of idealist absurdity. But all of this noise misses, or crosscuts, the central issue, which is, as it has always been, the place of revolution in the building of human freedom.

The following heuristic could be used to reveal the "political unconscious" of any work of comparative politics: First, when does the author date the outcome either of the "modern state" or "representative government"? That is, are these outcomes seen as the gradual culmination of secular processes such as "bargaining" (especially over taxes), or is there a strong sense of periodization? Second, how does the author deal with the question of the relationship between the English Civil War and the Restoration? Is the latter seen as the true path to representative government, while the former is treated as an unfortunate mistake? Third, does the author draw a contrast between a bad and chaotic French

Revolution and an orderly and stable English Restoration? Fourth, does the author distinguish within the French Revolution between a good, early revolution that lasted up until 1791, and a bad, later revolution? Finally, how does the author understand the outcome of revolutions? Are these interpreted exclusively as exercises in "state building" (see Skocpol) or, in contrast, are they seen as relevant to the development of human freedom (see Moore)?

Using this heuristic, the reader can quickly classify all works into two categories: more or less sophisticated neo-Burkean arguments, and more or less sophisticated neo-Robespierrian ones. Of course, this says nothing really about the intellectual sophistication of the work in question, but it brings out one important matter: the counterrevolutionary tradition is much more powerful than explicit references to its leading lights might make it appear. The worm of "continuity," "legacy," and "gradualism" has burrowed deep into the core of comparative analysis's image of history; the bias against revolution appears not as a political *parti pris*, but as a silent epistemological distortion, which makes it all the more powerful.

90

Negative space. What is the point of historical sociology? Is it to rummage through the past in search of examples? Is it to bring to light the origins of the institutional furniture that surrounds us? In these cases, the historical sociologist would be like an antique dealer: an expert in establishing provenance. The monotonous invocation of "legacies" suggests that this might be the dominant understanding, but such formulations miss the point. The purpose of historical sociology is to explain as precisely as possible why and in what way people's past actions mattered, which is not at all a simple business. It is a craft that requires a peculiar combination of theoretical and empirical ambition and restraint. For at the core of every historical explanation must lie a tightly circumscribed void that defies explanation. This is the zone of human freedom, in the face of which the "behavioral sciences" stand mute. No historically minded sociologist should attempt to explain action in this zone, for in the case of success they would eliminate the very indeterminacy that makes the occurrences there causal. Nor, of course, should they commit the opposite error of blathering on about contingency without properly historicizing and delimiting it. What one should ask is, What was possible at this moment, given this set of circumstances? This is just another way of saying that human reality is a structure of absences as much as presences, and requires a science of the negative as much as the positive. The deepest legacy of "positivism," one to which very many self-described "postpositivists" are fully in thrall, is the dogma that existence can be fully described by what is, without recognizing that the "is" is always the negative image of what could have been, and therefore contains within itself a series of absences.

In this connection, one suspects that too few sociologists have ever seriously attempted to draw. For the first lesson of good drawing is to train the eye by drawing the "negative" space around the object rather than approaching it directly. Invariably, the attempt to directly portray what one is drawing (a cup, a banana, an orange) produces a totem. This is because when the artist attempts to portray a positivity, a whole series of blinding, historically sedimented filters intervenes between the eye and the object. (The techniques of good drawing are in this way best understood as tricks to avoid the overwhelming power of commodity fetishism, so that one might see what is actually there.)

An analogous trap occurs with concepts. Enormous institutional pressures push scholars to frame questions as explanations of positively defined outcomes: for example, democracy "defined" as some combination of elections and rights. These "definition-concepts" are then draped over the cases; they either dangle off historical reality, or squeeze it into misshapen forms like so many ill-fitting suits. Most importantly, these totemistic definitions hide the background: in the case of democracy, that every modern representative regime was the outcome of the defeat of a more radical alternative. The Glorious Revolution of 1688 is not the republic of 1649–60, the constitutional settlement of 1789 in the United States is not the decentralized regime of the Articles of Confederation; the French Third Republic of 1871 is not the Paris Commune; the Italian Republic of 1948 is not the *via italiana al socialismo* envisioned by Togliatti. To define democracy as an outcome in terms of its positive attributes (elections, rights, separation of powers) is therefore a form of apologetics at the conceptual level that only serves to hide the defeated alternatives that every existing democracy carries around as part of what it is: its negative reality. Conceptualization, then, especially in the social sciences, is never politically innocent. There is a politics of concepts, which should not be forgotten.

91

Danger. The organic intellectuals of the Anglo-American university's sex bureaucracy focus on the problem of consent, which they see as particularly acute where there are large "power differentials" between the partners. Campus relationships between older male professors and younger female students are, for them, perhaps the key example of such power-distorted pseudoconsent; indeed, a truly consensual relationship of this type is now widely regarded as a conceptual impossibility for what might be called "Title IX theorizing." Doubtless, professors do abuse their position at times, but what is strange about the attention this particular relationship draws is that, viewed in the wider context of a deeply unequal and exploitation-riven society, it would seem to be among the least characterized by "power differentials" (although the meaning of "power" is never entirely clear in this discussion). Can the professor fire the student? No, he cannot; if anything the threat now goes very much the other way. Can the professor shape the student's inner desires? Surely in comparison with the vast advertising/consumption apparatus his influence in this domain is minuscule. Really, the professor has control only over two things: grades and letters of recommendation. But given that students can receive these from several potential providers, even this is at best an oligopoly power. So why the professor as a source of concern? The most obvious answer is that he (and in this context it really is a he) is an easy target. Usually lacking independent wealth, professors need their jobs. More importantly, perhaps, the professor is the subject of politically transversal cultural disdain. Perpetually adolescent, arrogant, out of touch, and unaccountable, he is a perfect object for the disciplinary project of bureaucratic "feminism." But this has about as much to do with fighting patriarchy as the IRS does with instituting socialism.

92

Lawsuits. A striking fact: discussions in both contemporary feminism and critical race theory are dominated by legal matters, and legal theorists are among their most prominent practitioners. Consequently, the social issues that they analyze are always converted into questions of justice, harm reduction, restitution of wrongs. Why is this so? Undoubtedly, it is connected with the massive ideological and political power of the courts in the United States. Indeed, the "juridification of the imagination" reaches deep into the historical theorizing of the progressive left in this country.

In these quarters, history is presented as a series of successive "social movements," loose alliances of citizens asserting their rights, that resemble nothing so much as class action lawsuits with a militant wing. It is as if for the United States, the Marxian formula must be revised: history is the history of court battles, rather than class struggles. The power of this imaginary, and its debilitating political consequences, should be recognized.

93

Clean hands. There are two great examples of the attempt to replace politics with what André Singer calls "the republican experiment (*ensaio republicano*)": the Italian *Mani pulite* and the Brazilian *Lava Jato*. These were efforts to create a political movement on the basis of anticorruption. The first ended in the spectacular failure and inversion of the Berlusconi years. The second was a decisive cause of Bolsonaro's rise, and prior to that Dilma's ouster. The two cases differed. *Mani pulite* attacked the entire political class of Italy's "First Republic," while Lava Jato, although paradoxically begun under Dilma, quickly transformed into an anti-Lulist project. But there is still a structural similarity between them. The "republican experiment" seems to emerge at moments when social democracy (if one can use this rather imprecise phrase to refer to Eurocommunism in Italy and the PT in Brazil) is in crisis. It becomes an alternative to the politics of redistribution. It as if to say, "Leave political programs aside and just ensure that politicians are not overtly corrupt." But these juridical attacks seem by a sort of quasi-natural law to redound to the benefit of the right, because they reinforce the impression that all political authority is inherently corrupt and should thus be starved of resources. The right, in this way, benefits from the common-sense "Marxism" of the "man in the street." Why should the executive committee of the bourgeoisie receive any further taxes? The task of the left is more difficult. It must, on the one hand, agree that the state is in thrall to the capitalists as a class, but on the other insist that a new sort of political order is possible. Hand washing and car washing will never answer the key question: "What kind of state?"

94

Roosevelt's soporific. The "Rooseveltian Dream," so Singer describes the project of *lulismo*: the attempt to "construct a solid and entrepreneurial middle-class country." In one sense this sounds surprising in the context of the United States, where Roosevelt is widely associated with public provision. But it quite precisely describes one of the major conundrums of social democracy. The vast majority of public expenditure under Lula took the form of support for projects of individual upward mobility and expanded consumption. This was certainly true under FDR as well, with federally guaranteed home loans being perhaps the clearest example. The political result of such policies is the fragmentation of the working class: its conversion into a sack of potatoes.

In this regard, to understand the probable future trajectory of the Biden administration, a close study of *lulismo* is likely to be of some use (granted the enormous political chasm that separates the two experiences). If the Democrats pass their huge domestic spending package, what sort of things will it support? Education, at both the pre-K and college levels, and health care will receive the bulk of the funding. But significant spending on public works seems wildly unlikely. The question that *lulismo* poses is, What are the political consequences of such forms of provision? The reinforcement of the "meritocratic illusion" (Singer) that is already a serious problem among US progressives. This is why it is important to insist on public expenditures that support clearly public forms of consumption as well. The political meaning of the Green New Deal lies here; if executed correctly it should create new solidarities rather than simply "pathways to the middle class" or "opportunity."

But the realm of culture also must be addressed. Here a break is required with decades of theorizing and research that conceives of culture as an individually held resource ("cultural capital"). Culture should be thought of instead as an irreducibly collective practice, producible and consumable only socially. Despite his overfondness for modernization theory, Habermas was certainly correct about this, and correct too that the Enlightenment salon in some way must reemerge if the public is to cease being a collection of "cultural consumers" and become instead "culture debaters." If public investment is made without such a change, the expansion of higher education will mean only an intensification of credentialing. It will also encourage the further fragmentation of the progressive base if not tightly linked to a transformation of the whole style of teaching and conceived purpose of the university.

95

Radical? It seems clear that a neo-MacKinnonite feminism is emerging. It would in fact be wrong to say that MacKinnon ever went away, as her particular conceptions have had a far more massive influence on social and political life in the United States than any of her peers. Her key idea is that expropriated sexuality is the basis of gender in the same sense that expropriated surplus is the basis of class in Marxism. But here of course differences immediately intervene, as Watkins points out. Most importantly, for Marx it is not exploitation in a generic sense, but always a historically determinant form of it that constitutes classes. For

MacKinnon there is one abstract and ahistorical process that produces gender: fucking. To take the MacKinnonite position seriously, perhaps more seriously than MacKinnon herself, should there not be specific forms of sexuality associated with specific gender formations? No such project has emerged from her. (Srinivasan, who seems to be a slightly updated and more moderate version of MacKinnon, makes little progress in this regard.) But,t of course, there is an even more serious critique to be made: "Why should one think that sexuality is the 'basis' of gender?" Surely, in a biographical sense people bring gender to sexuality. There are at least two alternative accounts that need to be recognized. The first is that gender is a product of the division of social labor between productive and reproductive (or caring) functions. Fraser's work is the most sophisticated here. The second is the idea that gender is the result of a process of classification, categorization, or performance. Butler's work is the key statement here. The MacKinnonite, or neo-Mackinnonite, position in contrast to these is basically a restatement of one of the key elements of US gender ideology: that gender is fundamentally about what goes on in the bedroom rather than what happens in the political sphere or in the labor process. Is a more balanced synthesis possible?

96

A parallel. Przeworski's famous argument about the "material basis of consent" leads to profoundly depressing conclusions. He claimed that working-class militancy is self-defeating in the medium and long run because workers are likely to be better off if capitalists invest the surplus rather than distributing it to workers as wages. The pseudo-rigor of the argument, which is made unnecessarily difficult to understand by an obvious typo in the discussion of the central figure, has perhaps contributed to its prestige.* But it is nevertheless powerfully presented. One might note, however, how deeply time-bound his claim is. Przeworski assumed that higher profits would lead to higher investment, which in turn would lead to higher profits. But it was precisely this dynamic that Brenner showed to be characteristic only of a particular phase of capitalism (the long boom). In a sense one could say that this discussion—which I have constructed here, since it never actually happened—reprises the debate between Bernstein and Luxemburg. For Luxemburg's central point was that what Bernstein assumed as eternal laws (especially the capacity of credit to stave off capitalist crisis) in reality only applied to a specific phase of capitalism. The problem is a general one: the attempt to jettison an account of history always ends up trapping the analyst in an eternal present that is more or less rapidly overcome by historical developments.

97

Spreadsheets. A hypothesis: the basic metaphors on which social theories build themselves are drawn from the dominant technological-social ensemble of the time and place in which the writer was active. Marx's concept of labor as the transformation of nature might be thought of as an expression of the first industrial revolution, the harnessing of coal and steam to human will. Weber's concept of rationality, with its central idea of predictability, is clearly reliant on the metaphor of the machine (the state is a machine, judges are machines, etc.) early in the age of petroleum, chemicals, and electricity. Durkheim is perhaps a more difficult case, but the obsession with the opposition

---

* See page 158 of *Capitalism and Social Democracy* where the text seems to invert $w^{\hat{}}$ and w^*.

between forms of solidarity, or solidarity and anomie, might be thought of as an expression of the peculiarly French polarity between a huge metropolis (Paris) and a sea of villages and medium-sized towns. (Perhaps nowhere else in Western Europe is a country dominated so completely by one conurbation.) Is there a dominant metaphor today that can be similarly rooted in a dominant technical-social practice? Undoubtedly, the key concept of contemporary social theory is classification. What does this metaphor reflect? What activity consists primarily in sorting information into row- and column-defined boxes, thereby creating order from a shapeless pile of numbers? The answer is clearly the spreadsheet: one of the most ubiquitous cultural artifacts of contemporary capitalism. And who is the social theorist who developed the logic of the spreadsheet into a full-blown social theory? Pierre Bourdieu.

98

False equivalence. (The reflections here should be linked to note 52 on class and nation.) An increasingly common expression is "classism." It is offered as an analogue to racism and sexism, but the assumed parallel is exceedingly strange. An initial, admittedly somewhat naive, objection is this: While at least a part of the substance of racism and sexism consists in attitudes or orientations to others, what do these have to do with class? Think of the implicit politics of anticlassism. Unlike antiracism, which might, one would hope, have the elimination of races as its goal—that is, to the extent that one believes that racism produces races— the elimination of "classism" as a subjective attitude has nothing whatsoever to do with the elimination of classes. It is quite possible to imagine a society entirely free from classism nevertheless being marked by deeply entrenched class differences. That is, classist attitudes might be eliminated, so that for example the children of the rich demonstrate demotic sensibilities indistinguishable from their less fortunate peers, while nevertheless remaining securely entrenched in their class position. Further, might it not actually be the case that an anticlassist sensibility is the "best possible cultural shell," to paraphrase Lenin, for capitalism? This is one of the major blind spots of the culture-and-class literature. For that work takes as an assumption that classes are culturally marked; but precisely this, the relationship between classes and "classism," should be a question for empirical investigation.

99

Universal estate. How should the fact of "educational polarization," the widening chasm between how college degree holders and non–college degree holders vote, be explained? The dominant position accounts for the divergence in terms of values. On this argument the highly educated are supposed to be open, tolerant, and cosmopolitan while the non–degree holders languish in parochialism and particularism. But this account is transparently ideological. It accords a universal mission to the professional managerial class while pretending that this class has no material interests. Conversely, the uneducated or "low-information" voter is condemned to the realm of parochial fantasy, above all fantasies about race. It is crucial to recognize, however, that university graduates have very robust material interests in the valuation of expertise, and in the expansion of positions to which their credentials allow access. Furthermore, the supposed parochialism of those without a degree often derives from very direct experiences. That both cosmopolitanism and ethnocentrism have their roots in material interests is extremely difficult to acknowledge in a political culture as suffused with moralism as the United States's is today.

100

A strong performance. The fundamental methodological position of historicizing totalization, and the sense in which such a perspective forms the self-consciousness of all specific social theories, is well exemplified by the current debate within feminism over Butler's concept of gender as performance. Butler says that gender is a self-denying, iterated performance. She thus seeks to dissolve what she regards as an intellectually dubious identitarianism that continues to haunt feminist theory. Arruzza's response to this argument is definitive. For she suggests that gender as performativity characterized by "the forced repetition of stylizing acts" is valid only in a specific period of capitalism: one in which, most importantly, leisure time is utterly dominated by commodified consumption. The methodological move on which the critique is based needs emphasis. Arruzza recognizes the power of Butler's analysis while at the same time suggesting its historical limits (and subterranean entanglement with commodified leisure). This is the basic form of critique at its best, at once generous and devastating.

101

Lost. The depths of the reification of consciousness in the contemporary social sciences should never be under-estimated. Recall that Lukács insisted that reification in classical sociology appeared both in the invocation of mechanistically operating structural processes understood as fate and in the conception of agency itself. The individual appeared as the calculator of chances within a context treated as given. Thus the reified consciousness is perfectly willing to give "agency" its due as long as that agency itself is individualized and calculating, and in that way of course fully determined by the social totality that appears immutable. The idea is action within constraints. Once the debate is set in these terms, interminable ruminations on structural factors versus agency can proceed. "Contingency" can also be introduced, usually in the form of some entirely random and meaningless variation that has huge subsequent consequences. (The rise to predominance of the QWERTY keyboard is a favored example.) The point is that "agency" and "contingency" are now entirely segregated from any collective effort to actually make history, especially to make history consciously.

The historical coordinates of this situation are obvious enough. The initial Marxist conception of agency as that which shatters the reified structure was of course the working-class movement: at once collective and self-conscious (Anderson). The disappearance of this element, or at least its recession, has profoundly shaped the methodological situation of the social sciences, which currently lack any plausible model of collective history making. They are thus left to wander aimlessly on the arid plain populated only by those strange fetishes: chance, structure, and calculation.

102

The tree and the river. The massive old gray oak broke the late afternoon sunlight into a thousand shards and scattered them around the patio. Muted voices and the soft clink of glasses created a complacent mood: a retirement, clearly. But whose? A "Critical Theorist." Then came the speakers. The first group extolled mostly personal and professional virtues: generosity with graduate students and dissertations, exemplary committee work, adeptness at bureaucratic machinations, fundraising. Following these came others charged with addressing "the work." They delivered speeches larded with references to Heidegger and "worlding," as well as some strange comments on "jointed buses" and their relationship to concepts. This was all received with polite, if perhaps mildly ironic, applause. Just as the speechifying was wrapping up, a river of porkpie hats worn by brightly colored drummers and trumpeters began flowing down the path beyond the great tree. It was another world, and yet almost close enough to touch. The impression was of an invisible yet impassible barrier between on the one hand the over-comfortable and one would almost say overripe world of the "critical theorists," and on the other the life flowing past outside. What creates the separation? Among other things, the paradoxical fact that "critical theory" has itself become an academic profession producing a professorial discourse laden with obscurantist idealism. One needs an invigorating dose of "What Is to Be Done?" after such proceedings.

103

Vico. With regard to substantive social theory, it is not difficult to state the difference between Marx and Hegel. For Marx, history is a history of modes of production. For Hegel, history is the history of states. At a more fundamental level—that is, in terms of their conceptions of what history actually is—matters are more complicated. Hegel formulated the basic problem: the relationship between *Geschehen* and *Geschichte*, between occurrences or happenings and their narrative causal ordering. Hegel thought these things were bound up with one another in a rather intimate way, so that what people did in the past was closely associated with what they said they were doing. But this general perspective raises a number of problems.

First, while people might provide ongoing analyses of their actions in the course of doing them, it is far from clear that they would necessarily understand these actions as part of a broader story called "history." That is, the extent to which actors or chroniclers are self-consciously engaged in "making history" itself varies historically. This is why Hegel begins his analysis with a discussion of types of history writing; these types vary precisely in terms of the question whether they are produced as a contribution to universal history, or not.

The second issue concerns the perspective from which a happening or occurrence can become a part of history, and it is here that the core difference between the Marxian and the Hegelian position lies. The Hegelian position always privileges the retrospective view: happenings become history when they are placed in the context of an unfolding story whose contours can be sketched only after the fact. The Marxian wager, in contrast, is that history can be made by the actors directly engaged in its making as self-consciously historical action.

There are several points to make about this debate. First, it really must be insisted upon that the Hegelian view, far from being passé, is very widespread. Cultural sociology (Koselleck, Sewell) is forever attributing causality to after-the-fact interpretations of happenings. These interpretations are then held to elevate the event into the rank of history. History is made, then, not by the people engaged in the occurrence, but by its interpreters.

Second, it should be pointed out that whether history is made consciously or rather through happenings that retain their meaninglessness for the actors is itself a historical question. This is why the famous expression about "people making their own history, but not in circumstances of their own choosing" is elliptical. For part of the "circumstances" is whether the actors making the history understand themselves to be making it.

The third point concerns the attempt to get a hold of the historicity of the current moment. The problem could be posed this way: whereas Marxism presented itself as the supersession of the Hegelian retrospective illusion in which events become history only from the perspective of "third parties" (philosophers), it might be more accurate to grasp history making in quasi-cyclical terms. From this perspective the self-conscious making of history recurs at particular moments: revolutionary ones. But in between these phases there exist more or less lengthy Hegelian interludes dominated by the cunning of reason, in which the retrospective view is at least relatively appropriate. In a general sense it seems that the current age is a Hegelian one: people are not making their own history, and they are certainly not doing it consciously. Instead it seems like historical events in this period take the appearance of blind fate: disease, floods, drought, fires. Even more, seemingly political events such as elections or wars appear to be determined by meaningless prerational impulses: anger, revenge, resentment. The task under these circumstances is to establish the falsity of fate in all these domains, to show how the "happenings" that appear as random are in reality the product of a confiscated praxis turned back on its initiators; in short, the task is once again to turn away from Hegel and toward Marx.

104

Accumulation. Can anything new be said about race and capitalism? Likely not. But perhaps a summing up is worthwhile. To begin with, we had better not, as Wallerstein and his followers are wont to do, identify the term capitalism with the history of the world since 1492. This particular night in which all cows are black has led to repeated dead ends. It is one of the many examples in the history of social thought in which overtowering theoretical ambition capsizes into blind empiricism. So, capitalism must mean at the least private ownership of the major means of production in addition to a labor market. This imposes a "competitive constraint" (Brenner) on owners and generates the distinctively capitalist search for relative, as opposed to absolute, surplus value; that is, capitalist firms capture gains from productivity rather than squeezing. What does any of this have to do with race? In the first instance, evidently nothing much. But if that were really true, then we would be back at the position that Labriola called the "theory of historical factors," or what is now termed "intersectionality." Capitalism would be thought of as one structure and racism another. Lo and behold, the two meshed somehow in Europe at some point during the fifteenth century. But this seems both implausible and unsatisfying, as if the history of racial thinking were somehow external to the history of capitalism. So, how to relate them?

The place to begin is to note two unevennesses that have characterized the history of capitalism since its emergence. The first unevenness derives from the coexistence within single national territories of capitalist and noncapitalist modes of exploitation. For the question of race, the United States from 1840 to 1930 is perhaps the crucial historical example. Here a powerful industrial capitalism coexisted on the same national soil as a clearly noncapitalist mode of labor control: first slavery, then sharecropping. What does this have to do with race? The argument can only be sketched here. First, wage labor generates as its ideological counterpart the notion of formal equality. This is obviously because only formally equal partners can enter into true contracts. Thus, the spread of capitalism is closely associated with formal equality in this sense. But slavery, and other forms of noncontractual labor relationships contradict the formal equality of contracts. In societies where capitalism is dominant, but which also include slave or other unfree labor forms, a contradiction thus appears between the ideology of universal formal equality produced by wage labor and the subjugation produced by slavery or other labor-repressive forms. The ideology of racial difference conceptually resolves the anomaly of unfree labor by dividing the world into different races, some of which are subhuman. It is for this reason that the firmest color line emerged in the world's leading capitalist power.

The second unevenness that links capitalism to race thinking is, in contrast to that sketched above, internal to capitalism as a structure of accumulation. Large fixed-capital investments tend to be laid out in relatively integrated and interconnected blocks (Brenner, Luxemburg). These investments increase the productivity of labor for certain regions for certain periods of time. The areas with the newest, most advanced fixed endowments come to be considered "developed" and the rest of the world "underdeveloped" or "backward." Thus, as Luxemburg suggests, capitalism is intrinsically uneven. It always consists of more and less developed zones; backwardness in this sense is a relative state created by capitalist development itself. Note that this does not imply that the backward areas are backward because of colonial plunder, however often it has been the case that such plunder has occurred. The process is a more general one. It is not a question of "dispossession" but a matter of unevenness itself.

How is this associated with racial thinking? In this instance racism becomes a lay theory that explains uneven development. The general point then is that "racism," rather than being a psychological disposition, is always best grasped as an attempt to explain the world, and particularly to explain these specific unevennesses. This is clearly what Fields means when she describes racism as an ideology in the Althusserian sense, in that it alludes to the world in an illusory way. The implication here is that the ideology of race as a "lay theory" cannot be combated through mindfulness trainings and online modules, but only through an alternative scientific theory that better explains the facts at hand. This is a theory that has capitalism and its unevennesses as its object.

105

Potatoes. Is the concept of Bonapartism of any use in understanding the politics of the current moment? To answer this question it is necessary to untangle some of the term's historic meanings. Marx's initial analysis in the Eighteenth Brumaire oscillated between two approaches. Bonaparte's rise was (a) either an expression of the backwardness of French society with its abnormally large peasantry, itself a product of the French Revolution, or (b) a regime of exception emerging out of an interregnum during which the bourgeoisie had lost the capacity to rule and the proletariat had not yet gained it. In the interwar period both Thalheimer and Trotsky toyed with the notion of Bonapartism, although neither developed an adequate theorization of it.

Paradoxically perhaps, the most systematic use of the Bonapartist model for the classic fascist regimes came from the liberal right during the Cold War: above all Hannah Arendt. In Arendt's hands the theory of Bonapartism was reelaborated as the theory of "mass society." Classes, said Arendt, no longer existed; masses did. But the model of these masses was quite obviously Marx's analysis of the mid-nineteenth-century French peasantry, which he had described famously as a "sack of potatoes." As an account of interwar fascism, Arendt's depiction of the collapse of class and of a mass society lacking in associational life was not at all convincing. In fact, fascism depended on a highly structured civil society, without which it could never have built its distinctive party organizations, and it emerged out of a ferocious class struggle.

Still, the notion of "mass" might be of some use, as Singer's work on Brazil shows. Among other themes he develops a version of the "sack of potatoes" thesis. Thus, for Singer, the paradox of *lulismo* is that its very success in combating extreme poverty was self-undermining, since it was premised on the expansion of precarious service sector employment; this form of employment isolates the individual from the class to which he or she belongs. There is thus a process of "massification" internal to the specific dynamics of capitalist development in Brazil. "A mass," says Singer, "is the form in which the class appears in politics when it is not organized as a class."

This raises a question: Have there been functionally similar processes of isolation, or massification, in other countries currently experiencing a Bonapartist phase (the United States, the UK, Italy, Hungary)? The answer would seem to be an obvious "yes," even if the specific processes have unfolded in different ways in different contexts. (In Italy, the rise of small- and medium-sized enterprises that emerged after the *autunno caldo* must be somehow related to the emergence of Craxi-Berlusconismo.) Two points are worth underlining here. First, the applicability of Bonapartism to the current moment is precisely what distinguishes this moment from the interwar period. It is almost as if the theory of mass society, which was inapplicable to its ostensible object, has suddenly found a phenomenon that it can explain. Second, it should also be said that the concept of Bonapartism should not be deployed to account for highly specific electoral outcomes like Trump or Bolsonaro. These are too aleatory for any such structural thesis to be adequate. However, the concept may be highly useful in accounting for the specific atmosphere in which the contemporary political struggle unfolds.

106

Labor. The distinction between productive and reproductive labor is crucial, but not always entirely clear. Productive labor is the activity of producing useful things. Its basic form is the transformation of a given material configuration into another configuration through the planned use of force. Reproductive labor, in contrast, is the labor needed to secure the conditions of normal human existence, including the conditions for production.

Two differences derive from these forms of labor. First, reproductive labor does not lead to accumulation, even if it is the precondition of accumulation. The process is best understood as the mediation by labor of two basically identical states. In contrast, productive labor always leads to accumulation in some form; there is always at the end of the process "stuff" that was not there before. There is always also a "mess"; this last requires reproductive labor to clean up. The second difference to be noted concerns the differing orientations to time that flow from the two forms. The time of productive labor is teleological. It unfolds in relation to a purpose or end state. More generally, life, from the perspective of productive labor, is a project. The time of reproductive labor is, in contrast, cyclical. It unfolds not in relation to a given that it seeks to transcend, but to one it aims to conserve.

It must be emphasized that these forms of labor are in practice intertwined. Marx for example emphasizes that every process of value creation is also a process of value conservation. Further, there are productive phases within reproductive labor; for example, the making of a dinner is from one perspective a typically productive activity in which the initial inputs are transformed through labor into something useful. But from another, food preparation is a reproductive task since it is meant to nourish and return the consumer to a prior state. There is still a general contradiction within capitalism between production and reproduction that plays out at every level of society, from the global ecological crisis to the intimate struggles produced by "second shifts" and "time binds" (Hochschild).

A key political question arises at this point. Would the humanized society be a new mode of production or, rather, should it be grasped as the subordination of production to reproduction? The two are not mutually exclusive, but it seems that the critique of capitalism that these interpretations support differs. The brilliance and persuasive power of classical Marxism derives from its claim that capitalism's strong point, its tendency to increase the productivity of labor, is also the thing that will bring about its decline, as overaccumulation leads to a sagging rate of investment and a lack of development. Thus, socialism could position itself as the heir to capitalism in the specific sense that through public ownership and planning a new developmental phase might ensue. In the current period very few socialists are likely to base their critique on this, productivist, ground. For one thing, no one has ever been able to convincingly explain how a socialist mode of production might produce anything like the developmental dynamic generated by capitalism. For another, who believes that growth is the answer to the problems of the contemporary world?

Still, some of the most convincing critiques of contemporary capitalism focus on its lack of economic dynamism, which seems to position the critics, if only implicitly, on productivist ground. Critiques of capitalism that begin, instead, from the contradiction between production and reproduction point not to capitalism's decreasing dynamism, but rather to its unsustainability. The problem with this sort of critique is that it easily falls into a rather aqueous Polanyism in which the capitalist productive engine is supposed to be reembedded in an expanded economy of reproduction.

As the entire history of social democracy shows, however, such projects of taming have never worked for very long, and have depended upon highly specific, and highly favorable, historical conditions that are nowhere in sight in the current period.

Perhaps there is a different way to frame the issue. Instead of seeing capitalism as a superstructure parasitic on reproductive processes (in nature and in the domestic sphere particularly), we could see the very opposition between production and reproduction as internal to capitalism. (This is Fraser's position.) The political strategy of a transition to the humanized society in this case would take the form of a progressively greater forcing of the internalization of externalities within productive units such that productive and reproductive labor would be carried on in the closest possible relationship to one another, and at the limit simultaneously. (The forcing might take many forms, such as continuous environmental clean-up, or communal kitchens and childcare facilities being located inside, and funded by the enterprise.) This would at the very least place severe constraints on the private appropriation and use of the surplus product. In that case the very concept of productivity would be transformed, together with the property relations that undergird it.

107

Jewish questions. It is widely thought that Marx said little to nothing about race. Kevin Anderson's work has to some extent revised this view mostly by focusing on his journalistic writings from the 1850s and '60s. But Marx's young Hegelian writing, particularly his review of Bruno Bauer's book, says something very important about race as well. Bauer famously argued that the Jewish demand for emancipation within Germany was contradictory because a Jew as Jew could not accept emancipation from a Christian state as a Christian state, nor could such a state give emancipation. Only when the categories of Christian and Jew were eliminated as political distinctions could both Jews and Christians be free as citizens. Marx of course radicalized Bauer's argument. He began by pointing to the fact of flourishing religious communities in the most secularized states in the world at the time of his writing (1843). These were the United States and France. Thus, he said, the Jewish question could not be resolved merely by transforming the state, or the political status of religiosity. It required instead a transformation of society: human as opposed to political emancipation. However, Marx shared with Bauer the premise that the solution to the problem of Jewish emancipation lay in the elimination of the socio-religious categories of Christian and Jew.

This analysis poses the following question to contemporary accounts of racism: Is it possible to eliminate racism without first eliminating the social category of race? This question is rarely posed, at least in the current discussion in the United States, and perhaps raises a certain amount of discomfort. Indeed, it seems clear that much writing on race operates within an antidiscrimination framework that is in important respects pre-Marxian, and in a sense pre-Bauerian. According to this framework an equitable treatment of different races is possible, but has not yet been achieved. There is talk of progress, lack of progress, backsliding, and legacies. But is it not much more plausible to argue with Marx that human emancipation requires not racial equality, or even an end to racism, but rather the elimination of race as a social reality? Would this not be the most radical solution to the question, given that it dissolves the very terms in which it has been posed?

108

Good conscience. The status of comparison in US sociology is being undermined from two directions. The mainstream of the discipline is resolutely monoglot and firmly focused on the study of the Land of the Free. It is unselfconsciously nationalist. Other societies are regarded as curios, their study a boutique luxury good largely irrelevant to the progress of the sociological enterprise. More recently a diametrically opposed critique of comparative analysis has emerged. Its claim is that comparison "presumes that social relations of power neatly overlap with the boundaries and territory of the nation-state" (Go).[*] The term for this presumption is "methodological nationalism." A couple of points should be made here. The first, and most obvious, is simply that a huge quantity of sociological research in the United States, even highly formalized work with many "cases," is basically idiographic: it concerns whatever has happened in the United States over the last twenty years.

The second point is that the critique of methodological nationalism is hardly compelling. There are very good reasons for taking the nation-state at a first approximation as the natural unit of society. Political systems, cultures, languages, class structures, demographic patterns, and economies tend to be at least strongly stamped by the nation-state container. Indeed, without this variety it becomes impossible to understand one's own society as a particular configuration of the possible. This is not to deny the fact of processes that transcend national borders: imperialism, capitalism, environmental degradation, intellectual community. But to understand even these, a national framing of some kind

[*]   Julian Go, "Decolonizing Sociology," *Social Problems* 64, no. 2 (2017): 198.

seems inescapable. Italian, German, Spanish, French, and English imperialism, for example, were distinct from one another, in terms of the classes that supported them, the methods of rule they pursued in the colonies, the economic meaning of expansion, and its geopolitical implications. One suspects that the function of the critique of methodological nationalism is not so much to provide a basis for better analysis as it is to offer a clean conscience to the unselfconsciously nationalist mainstream. Better, after all, to tend one's little garden, since anyway all the world is a single case, than to make risky comparisons provoking epithets like "essentialism" and "substantivism."

109

The ground of politics. Does the standpoint of sociology have a political meaning? Burawoy has tried to formulate the idea as follows. The object of sociology is a particular level of the structure: civil society. Sociology thus has a cognitive interest in the maintenance and extension of civil society, just as economics has a cognitive interest in the maintenance and extension of markets, and political science in the maintenance and extension of the state. Predictably, the proposal was met with howls of protest from the fanatically apolitical dead center of US sociology. It suspected Burawoy of harboring revolutionary sympathies, an idea that allowed the center to engage in the morally satisfying practice of neo–Cold War finger-wagging.

The real difficulty with Burawoy's argument is quite the opposite. The attempt to found a politics on the basis of a defense of a whole level of social reality is an inherently conservative position. Whence, after all, civil society? Burawoy is quite clear: it is a product of capitalism. (Presumably, the reason is that only under capitalism is the economic separate from the political; this allows for a sphere of interest competition outside the state: civil society.) Thus, to the extent that sociology is committed to the defense of civil society, it must be committed to its precondition: namely, private ownership of the means of production. This is, of course, a general problem. Any attempt to attach oneself to a specific layer or group within the existing structure leads inevitably to the development of an interest in the existing order. It is worth recalling here that what Marx thought he had found in the working class was not so much an "agent" as a concentrated negativity: a social reality that could only exist through the annihilation of the existing order. In this way Marx placed himself on the ground not of a positivity but rather of a structured potentiality.

110

Who speaks? The problem of representation is perhaps the problem of politics. The ambiguity of the term—to portray, and to act as the agent of—has been the focus of a great deal of attention. Perhaps the most valuable part of Bourdieu's sociology deals with this issue. What has not been sufficiently emphasized is the centrality of the critique of representation from the standpoint of the humanized society. The representative, especially of a subordinate group, always stands in an ambiguous position. She tries to speak on behalf of the group's interests. This raises the whole well-chewed complex of arguments about how the principal (the group) can control its agent (the representative). But there is a more basic problem that needs addressing. This is the interest that the agent has in the preservation of the group as it positively exists. The phenomenon is the reverse of what is usually called "vanguardism." Through this interest the agent is bound to the existing social order just exactly to the extent that only in the existing order does the group exist as a positivity.

Lenin described the phenomenon as "trade-union con-sciousness." What he meant is that the trade union leader, as an organizer for increasing the value of labor power, only has a function in a system of wage labor: that is, where labor power is a commodity. To that extent, the union leader has an interest in the maintenance of capitalism through his interest in maintaining the group called "workers." The role of the revolutionary in Lenin's thought is, in contrast to the trade unionist, to represent not what the class is (posses-sors of the commodity labor power), but rather what the class might be (the core of the humanized society). Du Bois discusses the formally very similar problem of the "race man": the representative of the race whose interests become bound up precisely with the reproduction of the race as it exists, and therefore of the entire society that produces it. Booker T. Washington might be thought of, in this sense, as a conservative "trade unionist" of race.

One can hear already the cry of "vanguardism" in rela-tion to what has been said above. But the charge is based on a dogmatic understanding of groups: particularly the idea that group existence is exhausted by positivity. But social existence cannot be equated with positivity, since it is shot through by what is not. The positive view regards the social world as a collection of two-dimensional totems with names such as "class," "race," "capitalism," and so on. But all such social realities contain their own negations as part of what they are. The working class in Marxism, for example, is crucially also potentially the negation of the working class, and indeed the negation of class as such. The question of which dimension of the class is to be pursued—its positive interest as a group of owners of the commodity labor power, or its negative interest in the self-dissolution of the class in the humanized society—is ultimately not a scientific but a political question. Similar points could be made in relation to any social category. Should the positive interest of the race be pursued, or rather its negative interest in not being a race? Should one speak on behalf or as the representative of women, or rather against the category of gender? Questions such as these show how the apparently most general and abstract ontological issues are in fact of burning political urgency.

Bibliography

Note to the Reader. This is not a formal academic apparatus. It gives no more than an indication of some of the texts I had in mind as I was composing these notes.

Adorno, Theodor. *Minima Moralia: Reflections from Damaged Life.* London, 1974.

Althusser, Louis. *Sur la reproduction.* Paris, 1995.

Anderson, Kevin. *Marx at the Margins: On Nationalism, Ethnicity, and Non-Western Societies.* Chicago, 2010.

Anderson, Perry. *Arguments within English Marxism.* London, 1980.

———. *Lineages of the Absolutist State.* London, 1974.

Arendt, Hannah. *The Origins of Totalitarianism.* New York, 1968.

Arruzza, Cinzia. "Gender as Social Temporality: Butler (and Marx)." *Historical Materialism* 23, no. 1 (2015).

Bakunin, Michael. *Statism and Anarchy.* Cambridge and New York, 2012.

Bauer, Bruno. *Die Judenfrage.* Braunschweig, 1843.

Bernstein, Eduard. *The Preconditions of Socialism.* New York, 1993.

Block, Fred. "The Ruling Class Does Not Rule: Notes on the Marxist Theory of the State." *Socialist Revolution*, no. 33 (1977).

Bobbio, Norberto. *Democracy and Dictatorship: The Nature and Limits of State Power.* Oxford and Malden, 1989.

Bourdieu, Pierre. *Distinction: A Social Critique of the Judgement of Taste*. Cambridge, 1984.

——. *The Logic of Practice*. Stanford, 1990.

——. *The State Nobility: Elite Schools in the Field of Power*. Stanford, 1996.

Brenner, Robert. "The Agrarian Roots of European Capitalism." *Past and Present*, no. 97, 1982.

——. *The Economics of Global Turbulence: The Advanced Capitalist Economies from Long Boom to Long Downturn*. London and New York, 2006.

Burawoy, Michael. "For a Sociological Marxism: The Complementary Convergence of Antonio Gramsci and Karl Polanyi." *Politics and Society* 31, no. 2 (2003).

——. *Symbolic Violence: Conversations with Bourdieu*. Durham, 2019.

Burke, Edmund. *Reflections on the Revolution in France*. Oxford and New York, 1993.

Butler, Judith. *Gender Trouble: Feminism and the Subversion of Identity*. New York, 2007.

Comte, Auguste. *A General View of Positivism*. New York. 1908.

Connell, Raewyn. *Southern Theory: The Global Dynamics of Knowledge in Social Science*. Cambridge and Malden, 2007.

Crenshaw, Kimberlé. "Demarginalizing the Intersection of Race and Sex: A Black Feminist Critique of Antidiscrimination Doctrine, Feminist Theory and Antiracist Politics." *University of Chicago Legal Forum* (1989).

Croce, Benedetto. *Etica e politica*. Milan, 1994.

Davis, Mike. *Old Gods, New Enigmas: Marx's Lost Theory*. London and New York, 2018.

Downing, Brian M. *The Military Revolution and Political Change: Origins of Democracy and Autocracy in Early Modern Europe*. Oxford, 1992.

Du Bois, W. E. B. *Black Reconstruction in America 1860–1880*. New York and London, 1992.

———. *Dusk of Dawn: An Essay toward an Autobiography of a Race Concept.* New York, 2007.

Durkheim, Émile. *The Division of Labor in Society.* New York, 2014.

Ehrenreich, Barbara, and John Ehrenreich. "The New Left and the Professional-Managerial Class." *Radical America* 11, no. 3 (1977).

Engels, Friedrich. *Herr Eugen Dühring's Revolution in Science.* New York, 1935.

Ertman, Thomas. *Birth of the Leviathan: Building States and Regimes in Medieval and Early Modern Europe.* New York, 1997.

Fanon, Frantz. *The Wretched of the Earth.* New York, 1963.

Fields, Barbara Jeanne. "Slavery, Race, and Ideology in the United States of America." *New Left Review* 181 (1990).

Fitzhugh, George. *Sociology for the South or the Failure of Free Society.* Richmond, 1854.

Foucault, Michel. "Governmentality," in *The Foucault Effect: Studies in Governmentality with Two Lectures and an Interview with Michel Foucault.* Edited by Graham Burchell, Colin Gordon and Peter Miller. Chicago, 1991.

Fraser, Nancy. "Contradictions of Capital and Care." *New Left Review* 100 (2016).

Gellner, Ernst. *Nations and Nationalism.* Oxford, 1983.

Gentile, Giovanni. *La filosofia di Marx. Studi critici.* Florence, 1955.

Gorski, Philip S. *The Disciplinary Revolution: Calvinism and the Rise of the State in Early Modern Europe.* Chicago, 2003.

Gramsci, Antonio. *Selections from the Prison Notebooks.* New York, 1971.

Gunder-Frank, André. "El desarrollo del subdesarrollo." *Pensamiento Crítico*, no. 7 (1967).

Habermas, Jürgen. *The Structural Transformation of the Public Sphere: An Inquiry into a Category of Bourgeois Society.* Cambridge, 1989.

Hayek, Friedrich August von. *The Fatal Conceit: The Errors of Socialism*. Chicago, 1988.

Hegel, G. W. F. *Reason in History: A General Introduction to the Philosophy of History*. Upper Saddle River, 1997.

Hintze, Otto. *Die Hohenzollern und Ihr Werk: Fünfhundert Jahre Vaterländischer Geschichte*. Berlin, 1915.

Hochschild, Arlie Russell. *The Second Shift*. New York, 1990.

Jameson, Fredric. *Postmodernism, or, The Cultural Logic of Late Capitalism*. Durham, 1991.

Jaynes, Gerald David. *Branches without Roots: Genesis of the Black Working Class in the American South, 1862–1882*. New York, 1986.

Kautsky, Karl. *Class Struggle: (Erfurt Program)*. London, 1971.

Khaldûn, Ibn. *The Muqaddimah: An Introduction to History*. Princeton, 2020.

Kolko, Gabriel. *Main Currents in Modern American History*. New York, 1976.

Koselleck, Reinhart. *Futures Past: On the Semantics of Historical Time*. Cambridge, 1985.

Labriola, Antonio. *Essays on the Materialistic Conception of History*. Chicago, 1908.

Lacher, Hannes. "Karl Polanyi, the 'Always Embedded Market Economy,' and the Re-writing of the *Great Transformation*." *Theory and Society* 48 (2019).

Lenin, V. I. The Lenin Anthology. New York, 1975.

Lukács, Georg. *The Destruction of Reason*. London and New York, 2021.

———. *History and Class Consciousness: Studies in Marxist Dialectics*. Cambridge, 1971.

Luxemburg, Rosa. *Die Akkumulation des Kapitals*. Leipzig, 1921.

Lyotard, Jean-François. *The Postmodern Condition: A Report on Knowledge*. Minneapolis, 1984.

MacKinnon, Catharine A. *Toward a Feminist Theory of the State*. Cambridge, MA, 1989.

Marx, Karl. *Capital: A Critique of Political Economy: Vol. I*. New York, 1977.

———. *Marx: Later Political Writings*. Cambridge, UK, 1996.

———. "Zur Judenfrage." *Deutsch-Französische Jahrbücher* 1 (1844).

Miliband, Ralph. *The State in Capitalist Society*. London, 1969.

Mill, John Stuart. *On Liberty and Other Writings*. Cambridge, UK, 1989.

Mills, Charles Wright. *The Sociological Imagination*. New York, 1959.

Moore, Barrington. *Social Origins of Dictatorship and Democracy: Lord and Peasant in the Making of the Modern World*. Boston, 1966.

Mosca, Gaetano. *The Ruling Class*. New York, 1939.

Parsons, Talcott. *The Structure of Social Action*. New York, 1949.

Pérez-Diaz, Victor. "Civil Society and the State: Rise and Fall of the State as the Bearer of a Moral Project." *Tocqueville Review* 13, no. 2 (1992).

Polanyi, Karl. *The Great Transformation*. New York, 1944.

Poulantzas, Nicos. *Political Power and Social Classes*. London, 1978.

Przeworski, Adam. *Capitalism and Social Democracy*. New York, 1985.

Reed Jr., Adolph. *Class Notes: Posing as Politics and Other Thoughts on the American Scene*. New York, 2000.

———. "A Neoliberal Alternative to the Left." *Dialectical Anthropology* 42 (2018).

Robespierre, Maximilien. *Virtue and Terror*. London and New York, 2007.

Robinson, Cedric J. *Black Marxism: The Making of the Black Radical Tradition*. Chapel Hill, NC, 2000.

Robinson, Nathan J. *Why You Should Be a Socialist*. New York, 2019.

Schmitt, Carl. *The Concept of the Political*. Chicago, 1996.

———. *The Crisis of Parliamentary Democracy*. Cambridge, MA, 1988.

Sewell Jr., William H. *Logics of History: Social Theory and Social Transformation*. Chicago, 2005.

Singer, André. *O lulismo em crise. Um quebra-cabeça do período Dilma (2011–2016)*. São Paulo, 2018.

Skocpol, Theda. *States and Social Revolutions: A Comparative Analysis of France, Russia, and China*. New York, 1979.

Somers, Margaret and Fred Block. "Against Polanyian Orthodoxy: A Reply to Hannes Lacher." *Theory and Society* 50 (2021).

Sorel, Georges. *Reflections on Violence*. Cambridge, UK, and New York, 1999.

Srinivasan, Amia. *The Right to Sex*. New York, 2021.

Sumner, William Graham. *Social Darwinism*. Englewood Cliffs, NJ, 1963.

Sunkara, Bhaskar. *The Socialist Manifesto: The Case for Radical Politics in an Era of Extreme Inequality*. New York, 2019.

Thalheimer, August. "Über den Faschismus." *Gegen den Strom*. 1928.

Therborn, Göran. *What Does the Ruling Class Do When It Rules?: State Apparatuses and State Power under Feudalism, Capitalism, and Socialism*. London and New York, 2008.

Thompson, E. P. *The Making of the English Working Class*. New York, 1963.

Tilly, Charles. *Coercion, Capital, and European States, AD 990–1990*. Cambridge, MA, 1990.

Trotsky, Leon. *The Struggle against Fascism in Germany*. New York, 1971.

————. *Terrorism and Communism: A Reply to Karl Kautsky.* London and New York, 2007.

Vico, Giambattista. *The First New Science.* New York, 2002.

Wallerstein, Immanuel Maurice. *The Modern World System I: Capitalist Agriculture and the Origins of the European World Economy in the Sixteenth Century.* Berkeley and Los Angeles, 2011.

Watkins, Susan. "Which Feminisms?" *New Left Review* 109 (2018).

Weber, Max. *From Max Weber: Essays in Sociology.* New York, 1946.

Wilson, William Julius. *The Declining Significance of Race: Blacks and Changing American Institutions.* Chicago, 2012.